FORERUNNERS: IDEAS FIRST FROM THE UNIVERSITY OF
MINNESOTA PRESS

Original e-works to spark new scholarship

FORERUNNERS IS A thought-in-process series of breakthrough digital
works. Written between fresh ideas and finished books, Forerunners
draws on scholarly work initiated in notable blogs, social media,
conference plenaries, journal articles, and the synergy of academic
exchange. This is gray literature publishing: where intense thinking,
change, and speculation take place in scholarship.

How Noise Matters to Finance

How Noise Matters to Finance

Nicholas A. Knouf

University of Minnesota Press

MINNEAPOLIS

Published by the University of Minnesota Press
111 Third Avenue South, Suite 290
Minneapolis, MN 55401-2520
http://www.upress.umn.edu

The University of Minnesota is an equal-opportunity educator and employer.

Contents

Preface

THE POPULAR VIEW OF THE STOCK MARKET has the proverbial "invisible hand" guiding the prices of securities toward a "natural" equilibrium. Stocks may move up and down for seemingly inexplicable reasons, yet many people assume that they will always trend toward the "correct" price, one that is based on the fundamentals of the underlying company, such as its current revenue, forecasted earnings, and plans for the future. Yet it wasn't until the 2008 financial crisis that many people realized that this toy narrative is a convenient fiction, one told to paper over the complexities and machinations at work behind the scenes. For the stock market is manipulable and manipulated, as scores of crises over the past century have shown. Traders on the floor of exchanges have been found to "front-run" other orders, pocketing pennies at a time that add up, over the course of days, weeks, and months, to a tidy profit. Today, algorithms move faster than the humans on the floors of the exchanges, conducting trades in microseconds and thus front-running the front-runners.

But this more complicated narrative hides its own assumption: that it is always possible to rationally understand the movement of the market, that it is possible to assign a cause to an effect, that the market can be transparent and completely understandable. Again, both narratives just expressed—the toy narrative and the more complicated one that takes into account market manipulation—assume that outsiders and insiders alike can explain why the price of a security goes up or down, why it rises to the stratosphere, tanks to the doldrums, or stays relatively stable. They assume that the primary things to be bought and sold are stocks and ignore other incredibly complicated securities, such as futures contracts, derivatives, mortgage-backed securities, and collatorized-debt obligations, the latter two of which were fundamentally intertwined with the recent financial crisis. To begin to understand the problem here, I must state the obvious: the market is composed of humans and machines. The machines are made by humans, and even in the case of fully automated algorithmic trading, these algorithms were written by people. And humans are anything but predictable.

Yet it is also the case that these machines are affected by a lack of predictability more fundamental than the human, namely, the noise of the material world. This noise cannot be understood simply as unwanted sounds or undesirable signals. I follow Michel Serres when he says that "noise is a turbulence, it is order and disorder at the same time, order dissolving on itself through repetition and redundancy, disorder through chance occurrences, through the drawing of lots at the crossroads, and through the global meandering, unpredictable and crazy."[1] Noise is the fundamentally unstable ground on which these machines, on which our human existence, stands. Order, then, is simply a form of appearance masking a turbulent noisy background. It behooves us to respect this noise as we try to make

---

1. Michel Serres, *Genesis,* trans. Genevieve James and James Nielson (1982; repr., Ann Arbor: University of Michigan Press, 1997), 59.

sense of the world, realizing that our models are but extraordinarily simple approximations of something that is constantly in flux. This is not to say that order does not exist but rather that it is transitory, always provisional and subject to revision. Our human order also appears out of this noisy background and can thus be different if we choose to arrange things in another way. So although this is an essay about noise and finance, it is also more than that, as I raise questions about the decisions we make to structure and configure our world in a particular way. I thus intertwine my close readings of the economics and finance literature with contemporary debates about futurity and possible trajectories out of the morass we're in.

For me, then, the market is merely the background out of which a more intriguing narrative arises, namely, the story of how we begin to deal with the complex imbrication of humans, machines, and noise. To make sense of this, we must delve deeply into the details, which is why I make copious references to the economics and finance literature. To help the reader in deciphering the dizzying array of terms, I've provided a short glossary and list of acronyms; more detailed accounts of our present moment in finance can be found in the popular press, including in *Flash Boys: A Wall Street Revolt* by Michael Lewis and *Dark Pools: The Rise of Machine Traders and the Rigging of the U.S. Stock Market* by Scott Patterson.[2] Although studying the market has always been challenging because of the complementary problems of observation and mathematical sophistication, it was not until the late 1970s and early 1980s that most financial economists began to realize that noise was an

---

2. Michael Lewis, *Flash Boys: A Wall Street Revolt* (New York: W. W. Norton, 2015); Scott Patterson, *Dark Pools: The Rise of Machine Traders and the Rigging of the U.S. Stock Market* (New York: Crown Business, 2013).

additional factor that needed to be accounted for. Noise upset their understanding of the market as entirely signal. No longer could prices be imbued with a "truth-value." Rather, the price of a security could instead be merely noise: "useless" information, often coming from less sophisticated traders. Yet like good capitalists, financial economists and traders alike learned how to profit from this noise, a profiteering that continues today via high-frequency trading (HFT) algorithms.

Over the past two decades, there has been a proliferation of studies about the market in the social sciences and the humanities.[3] Nevertheless, *noise*—sonic, informatic, or otherwise—surfaces only at the margins of published accounts.[4] I begin from similar conceptual positions to this work, namely, an interest in understanding the interference of humans and machines and their imbrication within financial processes. But I also wish to understand these situations through the reactivation of early 1970s philosophies, namely, those of Gilles Deleuze, Félix Guattari, and Jean-François Lyotard (in, for example, *Anti-Oedipus* and *Libidinal Economy*), as well as more recent elaborations by writers of theory-fiction, such

---

3. See, e.g., Karin Knorr-Cetina and Alex Preda, eds., *The Sociology of Financial Markets* (London: Oxford University Press, 2005); Donald MacKenzie, Fabian Muniesa, and Lucia Siu, eds., *Do Economists Make Markets? On the Performativity of Economics* (Princeton, N.J.: Princeton University Press, 2007); Donald MacKenzie, *Material Markets: How Economic Agents Are Constructed* (Oxford: Oxford University Press, 2009); and Trevor Pinch and Richard Swedberg, eds., *Living in a Material World: Economic Sociology Meets Science and Technology Studies* (Cambridge, Mass.: MIT Press, 2008).

4. Two exceptions to this are Franco "Bifo" Berardi, *The Uprising: On Poetry and Finance,* Intervention Series 14 (Los Angeles, Calif.: Semiotext(e), 2012), and Frances Dyson, *The Tone of Our Times: Sound, Sense, Economy, and Ecology* (Cambridge, Mass.: MIT Press, 2014).

as Nick Land and Sadie Plant. The potency of these writers' thoughts has been rediscovered through the recent debates surrounding "accelerationism," and I believe contemporary finance is the accelerationist example par excellence.[5] This disparate juxtaposition of methodologies, writers, and approaches is meant to reflect the elusiveness of noise, its stubborn tendency to escape any single theoretical framing. Noise is nevertheless constitutive of the market, a fact that financial economists and traders alike have come to realize, even if this understanding has been somewhat subdued in recent theoretical thought about the market.

I draw on three different forms of financial noise in this essay, paying attention to how materiality and the interference of humans and machines cause the meanings of noise to shift over space and time. In "Noisy Efficiency," I consider how, starting in the 1980s, the "noisy" activity of traders began to be a valid topic of consideration in mainstream finance and economics as a result of the apparent failure of rational models of the market. With "Affectual Noise in the Pits," I turn to the bodily practice of open-outcry trading to listen to how sonic noise in the pits becomes recuperated into practices of financial valorization, as affect becomes more important than rationality. In "Algorithmic Noise Producing Noisy Profits," I turn to recent developments in the intersection of computers and trading to trace how material practices of human-machine hybrids again enable noise to become a means for the capture of profit. The last case especially raises the issue of *speed,* particularly when the race toward risk-free profit turns into a race toward zero, and I discuss this in "Noisy Accelerationism" in reference to

5. Robin Mackay and Armin Avanessian, eds., *#ACCELERATE#: The Accelerationist Reader* (Falmouth, U.K.: Urbanomic, 2014).

the contemporary debates surrounding accelerationism. By tracing debates in the financial literature, listening to shouts by traders and sonic works by artists, and attempting to open the black box of computer trading, I aim to draw out the situations where noise causes a rupture in existing modes of thought; as the media theorist Joseph Vogl has noted, "in a crisis the noise of the system reveals its channels, its functional elements."[6] I attend to the elusiveness of noise as a concept, especially as it mutates between its existence as the dual of information and its embodiment within particular material practices, be they sonic, machinic, or something else altogether.

6. Joseph Vogl, "Taming Time: Media of Financialization," trans. Christopher Reid, *Grey Room* 46 (2012): 73.

Acronyms

AT
algorithmic trading

ATS
automated trading system

CAPM
capital asset pricing model

CBOT
Chicago Board of Trade

Ccru
Cybernetic Culture Research Unit

CFTC
Commodity Futures Trading Commission

ECN
electronic communication network

EMH
efficient-market hypothesis

HFD
high-frequency data

HFT
high-frequency trading

MiFID
Markets in Financial Instruments Directive

NLP
natural language processing

NSA
National Security Agency

NYSE
New York Stock Exchange

OTC
over the counter

regNMS
Regulation National Market System

SEC
U.S. Securities and Exchange Commission

TWAP
time-weighted average price

VWAP
volume-weighted average price

Noisy Efficiency

Noise makes financial markets possible, but also makes them imperfect.

—FISCHER BLACK[1]

CONTEMPORARY CAPITALISM IS IMPOSSIBLE without the contribution of information theory and the "cyborg sciences," as termed by the economic historian Philip Mirowski.[2] The discourse of modern economics and finance is rife with references to questions of "information": who has it, when they have it, how it is transferred from one location to another, and how it can be acted upon to realize a profit. Although Claude Shannon's work on information theory—and his sharp distinction between the signal and the ever-present noise that corrupts it—is our most well known exposition of information as a concept, in economics, the Austrian economist Friedrich Hayek had been pushing since the 1930s for a slightly different definition of information to be considered as the term for economic messages. Hayek's interest in the problematics of economic information was crystallized in his well-known 1945 paper "The Use of Knowledge

1. Fischer Black, "Noise," *Journal of Finance* 41, no. 3 (1986): 530.
2. Philip Mirowski, *Machine Dreams: Economics Becomes a Cyborg Science* (Cambridge: Cambridge University Press, 2002).

in Society." Considering a rational economic system, "*if* we possess all the relevant information, *if* we can start out from a given system of preferences and *if* we command complete knowledge of available means, the problem which remains is purely one of logic." For Hayek, such access is ultimately elusive, and thus prices become the prime medium of market information: "We must look at the price system as such a mechanism for communicating information if we want to understand its real function—a function which, of course, it fulfills less perfectly as prices grow more rigid." As the end of the previous quotation indicates, Hayek argued in his paper against price controls, such as those you might find within a planned economy. His policy suggestion would not come as a surprise to anyone versed in contemporary neoliberal rhetoric—because of the difficulty in collating all of the information in a society, centralized planning by a single actor can never work:

> This is not a dispute about whether planning is to be done or not. It is a dispute as to whether planning is to be done centrally, by one authority for the whole economic system, or is to be divided among many individuals. Planning in the specific sense in which the term is used in contemporary controversy necessarily means central planning–direction of the whole economic system according to one unified plan. Competition, on the other hand, means decentralized planning by many separate persons.

"Decentralized planning by many separate persons"—or algorithms. For indeed Hayek's watchers of the price signal are like little engineers—or governors—who keep an eye on the dials that reflect minute changes in information: "It is more than a metaphor to describe the price system as a kind of machinery for registering change, or a system of telecommunications which enables individual producers to watch merely the movement of a few pointers, as an engineer might watch the hands of a few dials, in order to adjust their activities to changes of which they may never know more than is reflected in the price movement."[3] Decentralized individuals acting independently on observed fluctuations in price: this is an approach that would resonate later with complexity theory but is written at a time in which negative feedback—the governor—has contributed to the winning of the war.

In the intervening decades, information technology expanded Hayek's dream of decentralized "competition" to the realm of the computer. For finance, computation is vital for *derivatives* and the other exotic financial instruments that are key to understanding contemporary finance. Derivatives, as their name suggests, *derive* their value from another security, such as a stock, bond, mortgage, or other commodity. Derivatives enable "hedging" of bets by constructing positions that, for example, limit potential losses. For example, a farmer might enter into what is known as a "futures contract" that specifies *now* a particular price for a given amount of wheat delivered at some date in the *future*. Although the farmer is thus limiting potential profits by stating a price for the commodity today, he or she also limits potential losses in case of a decrease in prices in the market. More recent types of derivatives include options, which provide the right (but not the obligation) to purchase (or sell) a given security at a given price at some future date, or swaps, which exchange future cash flows dependent on some underlying instrument, such as interest or exchange rates. The complexity of derivatives trading has additionally required the contribution of mathematically sophisticated financial analysts, termed "quants," as well as high-powered computers to crunch through computational models.

3. Quotations in this paragraph are from F. A. Hayek, "The Use of Knowledge in Society," *The American Economic Review* 35, no. 4 (1945): 519 (emphasis original), 526, 520–21, and 527, respectively.

How to determine a fair price for options was a difficult question. For the past few decades, options pricing has been reliant on the Black–Scholes–Merton equation, developed by Fischer Black and Myron Scholes and independently by Robert C. Merton (son of the well-known American sociologist Robert K. Merton).[4] In both of their models, Black and Scholes and Merton assumed that stock prices follow what is known as a *continuous time random walk* or *geometric Brownian motion*. The details of such a process delve into complicated areas of mathematics and physics (some of which rely on Norbert Wiener's precybernetics research), but in short, the idea is as follows. Consider a decision to take a step forward or a step backward, with your decision dependent on the flip of a "fair" coin: heads you move forward, tails you move backward. Even though the coin is fair, and you might assume that, over time, your average location will be exactly where you started, in fact, it is more likely that you will "drift" from your position to some number of steps away from where you began. What I just described is what is known as a discrete random walk; Black and Scholes and Merton considered a more complicated form that is both easier to work with mathematically and aims to capture more of the "dynamics" of actual stock prices. In the model, the random walk is in continuous time (therefore without the discrete steps of my simple example), the walk is geometric (meaning the random prices can never go below zero), and movements are based on sampling from the Gaussian or Normal distribution. Not only does the Black–Scholes–Merton equation depend on stochastic assumptions that resonate with work

4. Fischer Black and Myron Scholes, "The Pricing of Options and Corporate Liabilities," *Journal of Political Economy* 81, no. 3 (1973): 637–54; Robert C. Merton, "Theory of Rational Option Pricing," *The Bell Journal of Economics and Management Science* 4, no. 1 (1973): 141–83.

in thermodynamics and statistical physics from the nineteenth century but the resulting equation can itself be massaged into what is known as the heat or diffusion equation that is also well known to physicists.[5] This is analogous to Shannon's derivation of information theory; just as Shannon constructed his theory on the basis of the stochastic relationships between English words, Black and Scholes and Merton used the assumption of a random walk to construct their options pricing formula. In both cases, assumed "regularities" of human–machinic systems are simplified and codified to produce a manageable representation of reality. In the financial case, it would be of a piece with the simplifying assumptions underlying then cutting-edge financial economics.

These assumptions were vital to the two key frameworks then underlying mathematical finance: the capital asset pricing model (CAPM) and the efficient-market hypothesis (EMH). I will only briefly explain the CAPM, as the EMH is more important to my argument. In short, the CAPM relates the expected return on a risky asset (such as a stock or bond) given the so-called risk-free rate (i.e., the rate of return on an asset, such as U.S. government bonds, that is assumed to be riskless) and the expected return on the market as a whole. This is governed by the risky asset's beta (β), a factor that is meant to capture the relationship between the volatility of the market and the volatility of the risky asset. If the volatility of the risky asset is higher than the underlying volatility of the market, the beta for the asset will be greater than 1. Because there is underlying risk in assets with a beta greater than 1, investors in assets with higher betas will demand higher rates of return. The CAPM rests on

5. Philip Mirowski, *More Heat Than Light: Economics as Social Physics: Physics as Nature's Economics* (Cambridge: Cambridge University Press, 1989).

a number of problematic assumptions, many of which also underlie the EMH, namely, that purchasing or selling assets does not affect their prices, new information is available immediately to everyone in the market, there are no trade and transaction costs, and investors can lend or borrow at unlimited amounts at the risk-free interest rate.[6]

Cursory rumination on these assumptions will immediately invalidate them: not everyone has equal access to capital for investment, intermediaries charge transaction costs, information percolates at differential rates. Yet such problematics did not bother many economists of the time, partially as a result of a persuasive paper by a young scholar named Milton Friedman. In his essay "The Methodology of Positive Economics," Friedman distinguishes between "normative" economics, the description of what ought to be, and "positive" economics, the construction of possible testable hypotheses and named as such to reference positivism in the philosophy of science. Friedman further distinguishes, in the positive program, between the assumptions of a hypothesis and the attendant predictions the hypothesis makes: "To be important, therefore, a hypothesis must be descriptively false in its assumptions; it takes account of, and accounts for, none of the many other attendant circumstances, since its very success shows them to be irrelevant for the phenomena to be explained."[7] Noting that the assumptions surrounding the equations of motion for a freely falling object in a gravitational field are most definitely unrealistic on Earth, Friedman suggests that critiquing an economic theory on the basis of its assumptions is a logical error:

6. Donald MacKenzie, *An Engine, Not a Camera: How Financial Models Shape Markets* (Cambridge, Mass.: MIT Press, 2006), 37–67.

7. Milton Friedman, "The Methodology of Positive Economics," in *Essays in Positive Economics* (Chicago: University of Chicago Press, 1953), 14–15.

The entirely valid use of "assumptions" in *specifying* the circumstances for which a theory holds is frequently, and erroneously, interpreted to mean that the assumptions can be used to *determine* the circumstances for which a theory holds, and has, in this way, been an important source of the belief that a theory can be tested by its assumptions.[8]

Friedman's riposte against those who would critique economic theory on the basis of its assumptions has become standard over the past fifty years.[9] By making analogies with the practice of the physical sciences, Friedman's arguments are of a piece with then contemporary attempts to place the social sciences on more solid footing; indeed, Friedman notes that the inability of economics to construct controlled experiments is similar to the problem faced by astronomy.[10] In the introduction to a collection of papers on the EMH, the financial economist Andrew Lo used references from engineering (engine efficiency) and statistical mechanics (thermal equilibrium) to argue that "the EMH is an idealization that is economically unrealizable, but which serves as a useful benchmark for measuring relative efficiency," a statement that resonates with both Friedman's scientism and his understanding of economic hypotheses never being absolutely true.[11]

Further expounding on this aspect of the philosophy of economics will unfortunately pull me too far afield, so I will instead return to a description of the EMH to show how its own

8. Ibid., 19, emphasis original.

9. On why these unrealistic assumptions did not bother many supporters of these models, see MacKenzie, *An Engine, Not a Camera,* 9–12.

10. Friedman, "Methodology of Positive Economics," 10.

11. Andrew W. Lo, introduction to *Market Efficiency: Stock Market Behaviour in Theory and Practice,* ed. Andrew W. Lo (Cheltenham, U.K.: Edward Elgar, 1997), 1:xviii.

inefficiencies (as defined by the developers of the hypothesis themselves) lead to a consideration of *noise*. The EMH is dependent on the random walk properties presented earlier; if stock prices did not follow a random walk, the reasoning goes, then it would be trivial to exploit the underlying trend to make a profit. Eugene Fama, in one of the most well known expositions of the EMH, titled "Efficient Capital Markets: A Review of Theory and Empirical Work," argued that although knowing the distribution of past prices is important to understanding the distribution of future prices, "the *sequence* (or the order) of the past returns is of no consequence in assessing distributions of future returns."[12] Fama's exposition of the EMH considers three different potential informational efficiency situations. In the first, *weak* form of the EMH, the market is said to be efficient if it immediately incorporates information about past prices of a stock. The second form of the EMH is known as *semistrong,* and in this situation, the market is efficient if it incorporates not only past price information but all public information about the firm (such as company earnings announcements). The third and most stringent form of the EMH is known as *strong* and is when the market immediately incorporates all information known to insiders or groups who have special access. In sum, according to Fama, the evidence up to that point suggested that capital markets, at least in the United States, supported at least the weak and semistrong forms of the EMH and, in many cases, the strong form as well. In fact, Fama could at that point find only two situations when the strong form of the EMH did not hold. The first was corporate insiders in general, in which securities regulations already provided hefty consequences for

12. Eugene F. Fama, "Efficient Capital Markets: A Review of Theory and Empirical Work," *Journal of Finance* 25, no. 2 (1970): 387, emphasis original.

trading on this information. The second situation was "specialists" on the floor of exchanges, those who had access to the limit order book. As a result of this informational asymmetry, specialists could advantageously order trades to eke out small profits based on minuscule price fluctuations. While Fama suggests that this type of activity is evidence for market inefficiency, he indicated that it could be eliminated through electronic market exchanges, exchanges that were only under development at the time.[13]

The EMH, and, to a lesser extent, the CAPM, had become dogma by the late 1970s, with one economist stating, "I believe there is no other proposition in economics which has more solid empirical evidence supporting it than the Efficient Market Hypothesis."[14] Nevertheless, the EMH began to be attacked, not only for its inability to explain certain financial anomalies but also as a result of new forms of economic and financial research that paid attention to what were termed *psychological biases*; this form of research came to be known as *behavioral finance* and is linked to the early work of Daniel Kahneman and Amos Tversky in examining how people's expectations of future events do not match the assumed underlying probabilistic models.[15] As a result of this, a small number of financial economists began to ask how such inefficiencies—such as the inability to correctly estimate risk based on probabilistic models—

13. Ibid., 399n22.

14. Michael C. Jensen, "Some Anomalous Evidence Regarding Market Efficiency," *Journal of Financial Economics* 6, nos. 2–3 (1978): 95, quoted in MacKenzie, *An Engine, Not a Camera*, 95.

15. MacKenzie, *An Engine, Not a Camera*, 94–98; Daniel Kahneman and Amos Tversky, "On the Psychology of Prediction," *Psychological Review* 80, no. 4 (1973): 237–51; Kahneman and Tversky, "Prospect Theory: An Analysis of Decision under Risk," *Econometrica* 47, no. 2 (1979): 263–92.

might function within actual markets and whether they were a stabilizing or destabilizing force.

Perhaps surprisingly, one of the most cogent early discussions of these inefficiencies was by Fischer Black himself. In a 1986 presentation to the American Finance Association titled simply "Noise," Black constructed a binary between noise and information, suggesting that there were traders in the market who could not distinguish between the two:

> In my basic model of financial markets, noise is contrasted with information. People sometimes trade on information in the usual way. They are correct in expecting to make profits from these trades. On the other hand, people sometimes trade on noise as if it were information. If they expect to make profits from noise trading, they are incorrect. However, *noise trading is essential to the existence of liquid markets.*

As Black admits, his theory is not based on mathematical formalism and might appear to be "untestable, or unsupported by existing evidence," an oblique reference to Friedman's positive economics. But this does not matter: Black ultimately suggests that, in a prescient nod to later performative theories of finance, "someday, these conclusions will be widely accepted."[16]

For Black, the concept of "noise trading" is an attempt to rescue the EMH in the face of the "irrationality" of human actors. In a world that was governed exclusively by the EMH, there would be no potential of making a profit on information: market prices would instantaneously reflect existing information, making arbitrage impossible. However, the assumptions underlying EMH are not valid within existing markets, and thus those engaged in, for example, fundamental analysis can expect

16. Quotations in the paragraph are from Black, "Noise," 529 (emphasis added), 530, and 530, respectively.

to make a profit trading on existing information. Yet these traders must trade with those who "think the noise they are trading on is information." This implies, then, that the "price of a stock reflects both the information that information traders trade on and the noise that noise traders trade on." Black ultimately suggests, however, that even if prices incorporate noisy information, they are, for the most part, never more than a factor of two away from their value.[17] Black's distinction between "correct" and "incorrect" information implies, then, that over time, the noise trader most likely will not earn a positive return because of his or her erroneous beliefs.

Shortly after the publication of Black's speech, Andrei Shleifer (economist and early researcher in behavioral finance) and Lawrence Summers (economist, U.S. Treasury secretary under Bill Clinton, former president of Harvard University, and nephew of Nobel Memorial Prize in Economic Sciences winners Paul Samuelson and Kenneth Arrow) laid out the potential situations when noise traders might in fact do *better* than seemingly more informed investors. For example, unlike in the assumptions of EMH and CAPM, buying and selling securities is not "frictionless" (i.e., there are transaction costs and limits to the amount one can leverage in short selling), meaning that better-informed investors might not be able to take advantage of incorrectly priced securities. In these cases, what appear as arbitrage opportunities (as a result of noise traders pushing the price of a stock up or down) could be too costly for the better-informed investor. In fact, over time, noise traders and the informed arbitrageurs become indistinguishable:

> When they bet against noise traders, arbitrageurs begin to look like noise traders themselves. They pick stocks instead of diversi-

17. Quotations in the paragraph are from ibid., 531, 532, 533.

fying, because that is what betting against noise traders requires. They time the market to take advantage of noise trader mood swings. If these swings are temporary, arbitrageurs who cannot predict noise trader moves simply follow contrarian strategies. It becomes hard to tell the noise traders from the arbitrageurs.[18]

Shleifer and Summers, along with their colleagues J. Bradford DeLong and Robert J. Waldmann, incorporated these suppositions into two econometric models. One model showed that "noise traders can earn higher expected returns solely by bearing more of the risk that they themselves create. Noise traders can earn higher expected returns from their own destabilizing influence, not because they perform the useful social function of bearing fundamental risk."[19] Another model suggested that, contra the suggestion of Milton Friedman that unsophisticated investors will quickly exhaust all of their available capital,

> if a small number of noise traders are introduced into the population, their relative wealth tends to grow. Noise traders can successfully "invade" the population. In a world in which investors occasionally "mutated" and changed from noise trader to rational investor or vice versa, it would be surprising to find a population composed almost entirely of rational investors.[20]

This idea of the noise trader is now entrenched within the world of financial economics. Recent papers have, for example,

18. Andrei Shleifer and Lawrence H. Summers, "The Noise Trader Approach to Finance," *Journal of Economic Perspectives* 4, no. 2 (1990): 26.

19. J. Bradford DeLong, Andrei Shleifer, Lawrence H. Summers, and Robert J. Waldmann, "Noise Trader Risk in Financial Markets," *Journal of Political Economy* 98, no. 4 (1990): 706.

20. J. Bradford DeLong, Andrei Shleifer, Lawrence H. Summers, and Robert J. Waldmann, "The Survival of Noise Traders in Financial Markets," *Journal of Business* 64, no. 1 (1991): 17.

performed empirical studies showing that noise can become systematic in a market, correlated across distinct investors and subject to the same types of biases first shown by Kahneman and Tversky.[21] As Black surmised, the noise trader has become accepted by financial economists.

Indeed, the notion of the noise trader is additionally understood by some traders themselves. To come to grips with the economic and financial details of the most recent financial crisis, the writer Keith Gessen, in conjunction with the magazine *n + 1,* began a series of interviews with a person he calls "Anonymous Hedge Fund Manager" (HFM). HFM, embedded within the world of derivatives, arbitrage, and speculation, provided Gessen with an easy-to-understand primer on fundamental concepts that were obscured by a lack of in-depth discussion in the general press.[22] (HFM would eventually leave Wall Street altogether.) HFM, in a series of later interviews posted on the *n + 1* website, noted how market inefficiencies, produced through Black's noise traders, enabled the capturing of large profits during the Internet bubble:

> Yes, you want to be in an inefficient market, with "noise-traders"—people who believe that they have some skill but they really don't. A great time for stat-arb [statistical arbitrage] was during the inflation of the internet bubble, because so many people, so many average retail investors decided "I'm a stock market genius!" They were just crazy, they were just noise-traders that were creating a lot of distortion. They were sloppy in the way that they traded, and they were also doing things that were just

21. Brad M. Barber, Terrance Odean, and Ning Zhu, "Systematic Noise," *Journal of Financial Markets* 12, no. 4 (2009): 547–69.

22. Anonymous Hedge Fund Manager and Keith Gessen, *Diary of a Very Bad Year: Confessions of an Anonymous Hedge Fund Manager* (New York: HarperPerennial, 2010).

foolish and that created a lot of anomalies that stat-arb guys were able to exploit. After the internet bubble collapsed, that next year was a much tougher year for stat-arb because those noise-traders were gone. It's sort of effectively functioning like the house in the casino, the gamblers are all like that, when there's more of them you do well.[23]

Like Black, HFM understood the noise traders as being necessary for normal functioning. Noise becomes a vital component of the system, the unpredictable activity that paradoxically powers the equations that underlie modern finance. Additionally, HFM sees noise traders as part of a binary: those who have information and those who do not, the latter being the noise traders and thus able to be taken advantage of by those who trade on "real" information. Yet unlike Shleifer and Summers, HFM suggested that those better informed will ultimately be able to take advantage of the noise traders.

This distinction between noise and information is in the end, of course, untenable. All markets possess noise to some degree, as transactions do not occur without some friction, either in time or space. Noise is an undeniable aspect of trading as a result of the material, embodied world—embodied in the sense of humans making the trades or writing computer algorithms, material in the sense of the intersection of humans and machines within real systems rather than idealized equations. Noise, then, is not easily assignable to those who are potentially duped into believing so-called false information; rather, it is precisely a result of the factors just mentioned.

The interference between noise and information additionally arises because what "information" and "noise" mean to

23. Keith Gessen, "HFM Redux, Part Two," December 16, 2010, http://nplusonemag.com/hfm-redux-part-two.

these financial economists or hedge fund managers remains elusive. Although the EMH makes clear predictions regarding *how* information is supposed to be absorbed within capital markets to become efficient, it has difficulty defining precisely *what* information is, leading to the tortured attempts to cleave noise from information. In a world where people do not act like rational agents every moment of the day, where behavior is not predictable to infinite accuracy and precision, some form of noise is inevitable. In the next section, I discuss some situations when this noise becomes sonic, when information ceases to be quantifiable but is rather affective, raising questions as to how we determine what sounds, what noises, might in fact be information.

Affectual Noise in the Pits

> Specialists often cite factors peculiar to the floor, such as the ambient noise level, as important elements in their trading decisions.

> —ANANTH MADHAVAN AND VENKATESH PANCHAPAGESAN[1]

WHILE ELECTRONIC TRADING—and its materiality of multiple screens and ubiquitous Bloomberg terminals—has transformed the practice of contemporary finance over the past two decades, the sights and sounds of physical, open-outcry trading continue to dominate our cultural imaginary. The ringing of the opening bell at the New York Stock Exchange (NYSE), so cherished on the day of an initial public offering—the business reporter on the floor of the exchange, moving among the discarded paper littering the floor, weaving his or her way through the totems of screens and electronics, surrounded by the din of an unintelligible language—the shock of unexpected market movements captured in the faces of traders on the floor or in the pits, fear and anxiety that no psychochemical pill could relieve: these are the moments we recall in conjunction with the world of trad-

---

1. Ananth Madhavan and Venkatesh Panchapagesan, "Price Discovery in Auction Markets: A Look inside the Black Box," *Review of Financial Studies* 13, no. 3 (2000): 638.

ing, affectual moments that suggest rather than signify. Yet the trader's tableau is now primarily one of numbers, graphics, and text: the visual rather than some combination of senses, a single modality rather than the intersection and interference of multiple ones. Such images—for they are primarily images—are to be found in the recent independent film *Margin Call* (dir. J. C. Chandor, 2011), where the key moment of crisis is revealed through unseen graphs and values on a bank of computer screens. When drastic measures have to be taken in response to these numbers, endless rows of computer screens on the so-called trading floors are the primary visual accompaniment (along with the skyscrapers housing the firms) to the unseen voices on the phone that mark the decline of the firm.

This shift has taken place among a move toward algorithms that enable primarily electronic forms of trading as well as technological apparatuses such as the Bloomberg or Reuters terminals that provide ready access to real-time and historical financial information.[2] Yet the transition has not been without conflict and controversy, as the anthropologist Caitlin Zaloom has so ably demonstrated in *Out of the Pits: Traders and Technology from Chicago to London*. Zaloom's ethnography details how the Chicago Board of Trade (CBOT), one of the largest and most prominent derivatives exchanges in the world, and now merged with the Chicago Mercantile Exchange (CME), dealt with pressures to move toward electronic exchanges and away from open-outcry trading.

Because my interest in the sonic practices of finance is intertwined with open-outcry trading, I want to explain this practice in some detail.[3] An open-outcry pit, such as that found on

2. For more on the history of this transition, see Patterson, *Dark Pools*.

3. My account in the next few paragraphs draws heavily from Zaloom's work as well as documentaries such as *Floored* (dir. James Allen

the floor of the CBOT, pairs buyers and sellers through a bodily practice of trading involving extreme behavior. Orders to buy and sell a particular derivative, such as a grain future, stock market index, or bond contract, come into the floor and are routed through clerks to a series of brokers who line the top of the pit. In the case of the CBOT, the pit is an octagonal space with a series of raised steps. Hierarchy of power is reflected in position on the steps; movements of traders up and down do not come easily and are the result of actions by younger traders to raise their status in the pits, such as getting the attention— sometimes through physical altercations—of more experienced and well-regarded traders on higher steps. Here the metaphor of moving to higher rungs of a career ladder has an obvious spatial referent. Within the pit are traders of varying levels of ability and experience. Yet there are always those known as the "market makers" or "locals" in the parlance of the CBOT. These are traders who are not necessarily affiliated with large financial firms but who trade with their own capital. Their purpose is to provide market "liquidity"; that is, they are obligated to buy and sell contracts no matter the state of the market, no matter how low it falls. Locals hope to make a profit through *speculation,* that is, correctly guessing short-term moves up or down in the market. The goal is to not make a large profit by holding a position for a long period of time but rather to make a number of small profits through short-term holdings, sometimes on the order of seconds. Besides the locals, other traders in the pit are

---

Smith, 2009). See Caitlin Zaloom, *Out of the Pits: Traders and Technology from Chicago to London* (Chicago: University of Chicago Press, 2006), and for *Floored,* see Trader Film LLC, "About—FLOORED," 2009, http:// flooredthemovie.com/community/, and JCL's Forex, "Floored: Into the Pit—Epic Trader Movie!," May 11, 2012, https://www.youtube.com /watch?v=tCcxr-fyF4Q.

affiliated with particular firms and receive a cut of the profits through a commission-based system.

Because of the number of potential buyers and sellers for the particular contracts, getting the *attention* of a particular party is of the utmost importance to ensure the best possible price. Although garish jackets and ties, foam inserts in shoes to increase height, and physical heft provide some of these signals, hand signals and the voice are the primary tools of the trade. Particular configurations of the hand in conjunction with the head and torso present data regarding a potential trade; such signals are specific to the various exchanges.[4] Coupled with the hand signals are shouts of pairs of numbers, the order of which differs depending on whether the traders wishes to buy or sell. This din, this *noise,* presents a cacophony to an untrained ear yet a carefully constructed system to the experienced trader. Zaloom comments on these paired aspects of pit trading:

> The presentation of market numbers in voice forces traders to cope with the immateriality of the bid or offer. A number is rarely shouted once. Because each bid or offer hangs in the air for only a second, the trader barks the number into the pit repeatedly to make sure he is identified with it. At the same time he holds out his hands, fingers extended into numerical signals, to bring a concrete visual presence to his bid or offer. The sounds of repeated numbers form the cadence of the market and can convey urgency

4. Attempts are under way to document these signals as open-outcry trading fades in importance and is presumed to eventually disappear altogether. See Debrouillard Group, "Trading Pit History," n.d., http://tradingpithistory.com/. The futures pits at the Chicago Board of Trade Building, owned by the CME Group, were scheduled to close in July 2015. See William Alden, "As Silence Falls on Chicago Trading Pits, a Working-Class Portal Also Closes," *New York Times,* March 24, 2015, http://mobile.nytimes.com/2015/03/25/business/dealbook/as-silence -falls-on-chicago-trading-pits-a-working-class-portal-also-closes.html.

or boredom. In receiving the numbers that others bring to the market, traders appeal to "feeling." This word, encompassing all sensory information, is one traders use to characterize their knowledge of the market.

The body is a key interpretive instrument for the pit trader. Listening to rhythms of the numbers as they run in the pits leads traders to judge the market as "heavy" or "light," likely to rise or fall according to their sensory estimations. Beyond creating the basis for individual traders' economic judgments, the ambient noise of the pit affects the market as a whole. Economists studying the CBOT pits found that increased sound levels lead to higher trading volumes and foreshadow periods of high volatility in the pits.[5]

Zaloom's final sentence makes reference to one of the few academic studies regarding the role of sound in open-outcry trading. In the wonderfully titled article "Is Sound Just Noise?," Joshua Coval and Tyler Shumway ask whether the sounds of shouting in the pit (proxied in their study by the measurement of ambient sound level in decibels) might convey information that is not necessarily available on the computer screens that were then beginning to dominate trading: "we ask whether there exists information that is regularly communicated across an open outcry pit but cannot be easily transmitted over a computer network. Any signals that convey information regarding the emotion of market participants—fear, excitement, uncertainty, eagerness, and so forth—are likely to be difficult to transmit across an electronic network."[6] As Zaloom intimated, Coval and Shumway found that the ambient sound level of the pits *did* have predictive impact in a number of areas (such as the

5. Zaloom, *Out of the Pits,* 150.

6. Joshua D. Coval and Tyler Shumway, "Is Sound Just Noise?," *Journal of Finance* 56, no. 5 (2001): 1890.

"depth" of the market, "information asymmetry," and the "cost of transacting"). Their conclusion reads not only as a paean to the specificity of the open-outcry pit but also as a cautionary tale of accelerated moves to electronic trading:

> A key implication of this research is that in the trading arena, machine may not be a perfect substitute for man [*sic*]. Current electronic trading mechanisms are clearly not equipped to convey the kinds of signals for which a sound level is likely to proxy. Certainly computer terminals can be outfitted to offer some conveyance of nonmarket signals. But their ability to replicate the variety of signals that can be communicated in a face-to-face setting—for example, fear in a trader's voice—is likely to be limited. As a result, as trading volumes migrate to electronic exchanges, much of this information will be lost. The welfare implications of losing this information merit further study.[7]

Coval and Shumway clearly suggest the importance of *affect* conveyed by the noise in the pits via their evocative set of nouns: "excitement," "uncertainty," "eagerness," "fear." For Coval and Shumway, the intensities gestured toward by these words cannot be signified by changes in numbers on a screen. They note this via a particularly striking image: "For instance, a trader who tries to unwind a large short position by waving his arms and jumping up and down in an open outcry exchange might have difficulty communicating such eagerness across a computer screen."[8] Through a focus on sound and gesture, Coval and Shumway attempt to understand whether the situations they discuss provide actionable information to other traders.

Their interest in evocative sounds and gestures is of a piece with recent discussion surrounding affect within the human-

7. Ibid., 1909–10.
8. Ibid., 1890.

ities and the social sciences. An introduction to a series of essays on affect describes it thusly: "affect is found in those intensities that pass body to body (human, nonhuman, part-body, and otherwise), in those resonances that circulate about, between, and sometimes stick to bodies and worlds, *and* in the very passages or variations between these intensities and resonances themselves."[9] Such an expansive definition of affect is indebted to the work of Deleuze and Guattari, specifically their Spinozist concept of affect as a capacity or intensity between and within bodies. A key point of contention in these debates surrounding affect is the question of *intentionality,* or to put it more broadly, how much of affect is potentially precognitive or presocial. Here the interference with scientific evidence itself becomes a problem. For example, Ruth Leys has recently taken affect theorists such as Brian Massumi and William Connolly to task for relying on both an anti-intentionalist paradigm and questionable (and dated) scientific results. Yet Massumi noted in his touchstone work that affect is not presocial (and thus not anti-intentionalist):

> Intensity is asocial, but not presocial—it *includes* social elements but mixes them with elements belonging to other levels of functioning and combines them according to different logic. How could this be so? Only if the *trace* of past actions, *including a trace of their contexts,* were conserved in the brain and in the flesh, but out of mind and out of body understood as qualifiable interiorities, active and passive respectively, direct spirit and dumb matter. Only if past actions and contexts were conserved and re-

9. Gregory J. Seigworth and Melissa Gregg, "An Inventory of Shimmers," in *The Affect Theory Reader,* ed. Melissa Gregg and Gregory J. Seigworth (Durham, N.C.: Duke University Press, 2010), 1, emphasis original.

peated, autonomically reactivated but not accomplished; begun but not completed.[10]

Perhaps more appropriate critiques come from Constantina Papoulias, Felicity Callard, and Clare Hemmings. Papoulias and Callard note that there is a disjunction between the rhetoric of affect theorists like Massumi and the recourse to the language of definitive scientific evidence: "Even as affect theory shows how a biology of afoundational foundations can be imagined, the language through which the findings of neuroscience are invoked by cultural theorists is, paradoxically, often the language of evidence and verification, a language offering legitimation through the experimental method."[11] Hemmings, critiquing both Massumi and Sedgwick, argues that affect cannot be autonomous and therefore outside of social signification; in fact, it is precisely because it is *not* autonomous that it has political power.[12]

Following Hemmings, then, the power of the affective events described by Coval and Shumway arises from their very embeddedness within the structures of contemporary finance. One would not understand the wildly gesticulating trader as suggesting an adverse event unless one has internalized the means by which the market functions. Flailing arms in the pits become affective only when they are linked to the loss of money. Hesitation in a trader's voice is only accepted as fearful if one understands the context of the event. Though such affec-

10. Brian Massumi, *Parables for the Virtual: Movement, Affect, Sensation* (Durham, N.C.: Duke University Press, 2002), 30, emphasis original.

11. Constantina Papoulias and Felicity Callard, "Biology's Gift: Interrogating the Turn to Affect," *Body and Society* 16, no. 1 (2010): 37.

12. Clare Hemmings, "Invoking Affect: Cultural Theory and the Ontological Turn," *Cultural Studies* 19, no. 5 (2005): 548–67.

tive events may function in a fashion that bypasses certain cognitive processing, this can only occur if at some prior time the events were linked to an affective intensity. In this sense, both Leys and Massumi are right: the intensities discussed by Coval and Shumway might be more direct than watching numbers on a screen, but this directness only happens as a result of prior social and ideological interpellation.

Like Coval and Shumway indicate, it might be possible to augment existing electronic trading terminals to help convey "nonmarket" signals such as the ambient sound from the pits. Indeed, such services exist specifically for the day trader. Contributors to day trader forums such as "Elite Trader" have discussed a number of different potential sources provided by companies such as Trade the News.[13] These services are not cheap; Trade the News costs upward of $175 a month, and a new service called TrueSquawk has plans starting at $125.[14] Such feeds come directly over the Internet without the need for specialized hardware. These sounds additionally can come in much more complicated and specialized forms known as squawk boxes. Audio from the trading pits can be heard and controlled through equipment designed specifically for this purpose. They show up in fiction as well: in the novelist Robert Harris's recent financial thriller titled *The Fear Index*, the character Quarry, at a pivotal moment in the narrative when his firm's automated trading system begins to go awry, "pressed a switch and picked up the live audio feed from the pit of the

13. Elite Trader Forums, "Forum—Floor Squawk Box?," August 23, 2006, http://www.elitetrader.com/vb/showthread.php?threadid=75425.

14. TrueSquawk, "TrueSquawk.com Live Futures Coverage," 2015, http://www.truesquawk.com/; TradeTheNews.com, "Live Stock Market Forex News Expert Market Analysis—TradeTheNews.com," February 9, 2015, http://www.tradethenews.com/.

S&P500 in Chicago. It was a service they subscribed to. It gave them an immediate feel for the market you couldn't always get just from the figures."[15]

Other types of "squawk boxes" have had more pernicious effects. Rather than a feed of sounds and commentary from the pits, squawk boxes within large firms are "internal intercom systems used by broker-dealers to broadcast institutional customer order information to traders and sales traders at the broker-dealer."[16] In other words, these squawk boxes are basically continually open intercoms that enable employees at the firm to assist with customer trading activity without having to continually retelephone others who might be able to help. On reflection, access to the content of these conversations could be extremely useful for investors outside of the firm, as it would provide information about potentially large upcoming movements in a particular financial instrument.[17] In 2007, Merrill Lynch was sanctioned by the U.S. Securities and Exchange Commission (SEC) for providing unaffiliated day traders with unauthorized access to these squawk box feeds:

> The [Merrill Lynch] retail brokers called the day trading firm and placed their telephone receiver next to the equity squawk box for the entire trading day. As a result, the day traders received real-time access to the equity squawk box and the confidential

15. Robert Harris, *The Fear Index* (New York: Alfred A. Knopf, 2012), 198. To my knowledge, further academic studies regarding the use—or nonuse—of these squawk boxes does not exist.

16. Tracy Alloway, "More Bad News from Merrill, Squawkbox Edition," March 11, 2009, http://ftalphaville.ft.com/blog/2009/03/11/53471/more-bad-news-from-merrill-squawkbox-edition/.

17. For more on the use of the telephone in trading, see Fabian Muniesa, "Trading-Room Telephones and the Identification of Counterparts," in Pinch and Swedberg, *Living in a Material World*, 291–313.

order information transmitted over it. The day traders compensated the brokers for access to the confidential order information through kickbacks in the form of commissions and cash. The day traders used the information to trade ahead of the customer orders and many times profited when the price of the security moved in their favor because of the market impact of the institutional customer orders.[18]

Merrill Lynch was forced to pay a fine of $7 million and implement appropriate controls over any future access to a squawk box or "squawk-related technology."[19] This particular SEC action was prior to the most recent financial crises; however, access to these types of squawk boxes was also a key sticking point in attempts to strengthen regulations in the wake of revelations over inappropriate derivatives transactions. Because most of the volume (in numbers of trades and in size of the position) of exotic derivatives contracts still takes place over the counter (OTC), or through lightly regulated transactions between individual entities, and not on an open market, squawk boxes have been considered a necessary component of trading to discover the current prices for these instruments. Yet like the move from open-outcry trading to electronic exchanges, a similar move has been suggested for most OTC derivatives contracts—a move that would silence these types of squawk boxes as well—in the name of market transparency: "The more transparent a marketplace, the more liquid it is, the more competitive it is and the lower the costs for corporations that use derivatives to hedge their risks."[20] Paradoxically, however, these

18. U.S. Securities and Exchange Commission, "Administrative Proceeding Release No. 34-59555," March 11, 2007, 3.

19. Ibid., 7.

20. Gary Gensler, then chairman of the U.S. Commodity Futures Trading Commission (CFTC), quoted in Michael Mackenzie and Aline

changes in the regulatory environment will perhaps silence the very signals—in digital form yet unquantifiable—that contribute to the transparency so desired.

Taken together, these cases of affectual sonic noise function within varied situations of human responses to the dynamics of systems. The fields of individual traders and the market interfere during temporal conjunctions where orderly operation breaks down: interference becomes sonic, a signal that can precipitate further action. Information and affect intertwine, becoming difficult to disentangle. As the pace of trading increases, however, affectual sounds can only be directed toward past events, toward the noise of computational processes that produce their own conditions for the accumulation of profit or loss.

van Duyn, "Regulators May Silence Derivative Squawk Boxes," *Financial Times*, July 21, 2010, http://www.ft.com/intl/cms/s/0/cce3f6e4-94f8 -11df-af3b-00144feab49a.html.

Algorithmic Noise Producing Noisy Profits

> A price of a trade is not a noisy observation: We introduce
> noise only as a mathematical idealization.
>
> —IONUT FLORESCU[1]

IN MAHWAH, NEW JERSEY, next to a car dealership and across State
Route 17 from a Home Depot, sits 1700 MacArthur Boulevard,
what appears on Google Maps to be a relatively nondescript
large, rectangular building, seemingly identical to scores of
similar ones within this part of New Jersey. Zooming in closer,
we can see, however, a rather imposing guardhouse and what
appears to be a number of hefty pop-up barriers to prevent
speeding vehicles, a self-contained electrical substation, and a
massive number of air-conditioning units surrounded by an ex-

---

1. Ionut Florescu, as quoted in Frank J. Fabozzi, Sergio M. Focardi,
and Caroline Jonas, "High-Frequency Trading: Methodologies and
Market Impact," *Review of Futures Markets* 19 (2011): 13.

tremely tall fence—all details that mark this building as other, as something special. A little bit of online searching reveals that this address is the location of the NYSE's newest data center, a four hundred thousand square foot facility.[2] The decrease in importance of open-outcry trading is imbricated with the increase in the importance of electronic market exchanges and electronic access to market information. New trading "floors" become the norm, this time populated by racks of servers in rooms of the most carefully controlled climate. Instead of the chaos and noise of shouted trades on the human-populated trading floor, we have the hum and white noise of air conditioning and whirring fans. Yet an additional type of noise can be found, one that resonates with the noise traders discussed earlier.

Zaloom's book detailed the conflicts over this transition from primarily human to primarily computational markets, and it is safe to say that today, the primary location of high finance is not 11 Wall Street in New York City or 141 West Jackson Boulevard in Chicago (the address of the CBOT) but rather 1700 MacArthur Boulevard in Mahwah, New Jersey, or 1400 Federal Boulevard in Carteret, New Jersey (the site of the NASDAQ's leased data center). A variety of sociotechnical shifts enabled this move to take place, including the move to decimalization in market prices, wider availability of powerful commodity com-

---

2. Anonymous, "1Q 2010 NJ Office, Industrial Markets Mixed," April 14, 2010, http://newyork.citybizlist.com/article/1q-2010-nj-office -industrial-markets-mixed-0. As far as I am able to discover, only the name of the city, but not this exact address, appears on the website of the NYSE. The size of the NYSE data center puts it on par with those recently built by Apple, Facebook, and the data center under construction in Utah for the NSA; on the latter, see James Bamford, "The NSA Is Building the Country's Biggest Spy Center (Watch What You Say)," March 15, 2012, http://www.wired.com/threatlevel/2012/03/ff_nsadatacenter/all/1.

putational technologies, and regulatory changes that opened exchange trading to more potential firms. Facilities like 1700 MacArthur Boulevard reflect important changes in the financial landscape, changes that are intimately related—yet perhaps are more impactful over the long run—to the proliferation of the exotic accumulators of profit that were some of the primary causes of the most recent financial crisis. Key to this whole field is electronic trading. In the United States, electronic trading in some form has been around since at least 1971, the year of the NASDAQ's founding. Throughout the intervening decades, exchanges—and the ways in which traders interact with the exchanges—have become increasingly electronic and digital.[3] Though low-latency access to information through computer terminals such as those produced by Bloomberg and Reuters have in part changed the way traders interact with the market, arguably more fundamental shifts have occurred through the development of purely electronic communication networks (ECNs), with names that fly below the public's radar, such as BATS in the United States and Chi-X Europe.[4] The development of these exchanges was in part enabled through regulations such as the Regulation National Market System (regNMS) in the United States and the Markets in Financial Instruments Directive (MiFID) in Europe, both of a piece with larger processes of liberalization existing since the 1970s. As anthropologist Marc Lenglet notes, MiFID restructured markets to both enhance the "competition between execution venues" and protect customers from the "'natural' dangers they may encounter

3. For one history of this development, see Patterson, *Dark Pools*.

4. http://www.batstrading.com/ and https://www.batstrading.co.uk/about/. BATS now owns Chi-X Europe, which is separate from Chi-X Global.

in markets."[5] Such ECNs are accessible not only through human interaction but also through automated trading systems (ATSs), thereby enabling purely electronic trading and thus the development of algorithmic trading (AT).[6]

Efficiency is again the standard answer given for AT. If an individual like myself wanted to sell, say, ten shares, I once could do so with the reasonable expectation that the price will not decrease during the time that I made this transaction. But consider the institutional customer who wishes, for whatever reason, to sell one hundred thousand shares. Such a move would almost certainly cause the price of the security to decrease while the transaction was taking place. Perhaps there would not even *be* one hundred thousand corresponding buy orders. These kinds of situations, of course, invalidate some of the general assumptions of the EMH and CAPM (briefly discussed in the first section), namely, that buying or selling a security does not impact its price. AT developed in part to deal with this conundrum. Rather than selling all hundred thousand shares at once, a specially designed algorithm could split this order into smaller pieces—say, twenty-five thousand shares at a time—to cause a smaller impact on the market. This process of selling could then be programmed to take place over a given time

5. Marc Lenglet, "Conflicting Codes and Codings," *Theory, Culture, and Society* 28, no. 6 (2011): 48.

6. For more on these shifts in the equity markets, see Dave Cliff, Dan Brown, and Philip Treleaven, "Technology Trends in the Financial Markets: A 2020 Vision," *Future of Computer Trading in Financial Markets—Foresight Driver Review* DR 3 (2010): 5–14; for derivatives markets in the United States, see Thomas J. McCool and Cecile O. Trop, *Commodity Exchange Act: Issues Related to the Regulation of Electronic Trading Systems,* General Accounting Office report GGD-00-99 (Washington, D.C.: Government Printing Office, 2000), http://www.gao .gov/assets/230/229069.pdf.

frame, say, an hour. Such an algorithm is called time-weighted average price (TWAP). But perhaps the security is rather illiquid; there might only be fifteen thousand shares being traded on average per hour. An order to sell twenty-five thousand shares in an hour, then, would have an adverse impact. Trades could then be cut into smaller pieces based on the historical pattern of volume for the given security; the goal would be not to cause an appreciable impact on the volume by the trade. This type of algorithm is termed volume-weighted average price (VWAP). Current algorithms used in AT have become progressively more complicated, taking into account more aspects of market dynamics, such as changes in the market during the execution of the algorithm, as well as attempting to position and time trades based on natural language processing (NLP) of recently released news articles.[7] The financial economists Peter Gomber, Björn Arndt, Marco Lutat, and Tim Uhle thus describe the characteristics of AT as follows: it is trading on behalf of clients, its goal is to minimize market impact, positions are held for relatively long periods, the goal is to match a particular predefined benchmark, and a given order is executed over a particular time frame and across a number of markets.[8]

It becomes easy to foresee how algorithms such as those just described could become ever more complex, absent negative regulatory pressures or lack of engineering wherewithal. Given that the space of potential market algorithms is practically unlimited, it is unsurprising to find out that there has developed, in the words of an official from the Bank of England, a "race to zero" that has pushed both time frames and complexity beyond

7. Peter Gomber, Björn Arndt, Marco Lutat, and Tim Uhle, "High-Frequency Trading," working paper commissioned by the Deutsche Börse Group, 2011, 21–23.

8. Ibid., 14.

normal human comprehension.[9] These new types of algorithms are termed in general HFT and have come under intense scrutiny for reasons that will become clear in a moment.

Before explaining some of the more prominent HFT algorithms, we have to step back a bit to examine the infrastructure that has in part enabled them to exist. Besides the establishment of new exchanges like BATS and Chi-X Europe, there has been the expansion of electronic trading activities at more established exchanges such as the NYSE and the CBOT, resulting in the building of data centers such as the one at 1700 MacArthur Boulevard. Overall, this has led to a pushing of computational limits as firms with immense levels of capital hire computer engineers and purchase specialized equipment to ensure that their algorithms are microseconds faster. For example, *colocation* is one of the latest trends in electronic trading. Although light traveling down fiber-optic cables is fast, it is not instantaneous. Therefore one of the reasons for the size of the NYSE data center is to provide rack spaces for interested firms (who possess both the expertise to manage the systems and capital to pay the fees) to be closer to the actual machines executing the trades. Evidently, much effort goes into ensuring that servers in racks nearest those running the trading system do not have an advantage over those located a bit farther away, even going so far as to ensure that all cable lengths are the same.[10] For those unable or un-

9. Andrew G. Haldane, "The Race to Zero," speech given to the International Economic Association Sixteenth World Congress, Beijing, China, July 8, 2011, http://www.bankofengland.co.uk/archive/Documents/historicpubs/speeches/2011/speech509.pdf.

10. Donald MacKenzie, "How to Make Money in Microseconds," *London Review of Books* 33, no. 10 (2011): 16–18; J. Doyne Farmer and Spyros Skouras, "An Ecological Perspective on the Future of Computer

willing to co-locate their servers, straighter and faster fiber-optic lines have been laid between New Jersey and Chicago by a company called Spread Networks, enabling them both to cut three milliseconds off the previous time (or distance) *and* to describe their distance from a New Jersey data center and the NASDAQ as "8 microseconds away."[11] Even faster connections now exist between the NYSE and the NASDAQ through laser transmission that shaves nanoseconds off the previous trip over fiber-optic or microwave links.[12] Injecting a bit of seeming science fiction into the mix are attempts to take into account *relativistic* conditions to choose the optimum placement of new data centers with respect to existing ones so as to create potential arbitrage opportunities, raising troubling regulatory issues in the process.[13] And data centers, although relatively "self-sufficient" in the sense that they have extensive systems for electrical backup, are still reliant on extraordinarily precise timing provided by GPS signals. Such signals, though originating from geostationary satellites, can be spoofed by a more powerful signal closer to the receiver. Some

---

Trading," *Future of Computer Trading in Financial Markets—Foresight Driver Review* DR 6 (2010).

11. Spread Networks, "Spread Networks® Collocation Centers," specifications sheet, 2011, 2.

12. Sebastian Anthony, "New Laser Network between NYSE and NASDAQ Will Allow High-Frequency Traders to Make Even More Money," *Extreme Tech* (blog), February 14, 2014, http://www.extremetech.com/extreme/176551-new-laser-network-between-nyse-and-nasdaq-will-allow-high-frequency-traders-to-make-even-more-money.

13. A. D. Wissner-Gross and C. E. Freer, "Relativistic Statistical Arbitrage," *Physical Review E* 82, no. 5 (2010): 056104; James J. Angel, "Impact of Special Relativity on Securities Regulation," *Future of Computer Trading in Financial Markets—Foresight Driver Review* DR 15 (2011).

have suggested that such jamming could cause havoc for financial organizations dependent on HFT, potentially causing timing confusion that could have a ripple effect throughout a market.[14]

This sort of infrastructural investment, couched in the language of financial return, must enable firms that engage in this work to capture some additional bit of profit that would not otherwise be possible. So why might these properties—of low latency, of close proximity to market computers—be so attractive? There must be a separate logic at work than with AT, as the AT algorithms previously discussed do not necessarily depend on *speed*. It is precisely minuscule fluctuations in price—a form of noise to which I will return shortly—that enable HFT to command so much attention in today's financial climate. In contrast to the qualities of AT described earlier, HFT involves an extremely high number of bids or asks, rapid cancelation of existing orders, proprietary trading, capture of spreads, no desire to hold a position for a long period of time (thus meaning that positions are held on the order of minutes or seconds or less rather than days, months, or years), and very low margins.[15] We can now understand a bit why the question of *location* is key to HFT. Given the material limits of communication networks, and assuming all else is equal, it is a truism that it will take longer for data to travel between a machine in New Jersey and one in Chicago than it will to travel between two machines in the same data center in New Jersey. Therefore, if an algorithm can take advantage of this latency delay, then it might be possible to enact some sort of arbitrage opportunity. For example, HFTs

14. Olivia Solon, "GPS 'Spoofers' Could Be Used for High-Frequency Financial Trading Fraud," *Wired*, February 22, 2012, http://www.wired.co.uk/news/archive/2012-02/22/gps-spoofing.

15. Gomber et al., "High-Frequency Trading," 15.

might work as a market maker (described earlier in the context of open-outcry trading) to capture the spread between the bid and the ask, an activity that offers very low returns for each trade but can add up to large profits over time. In the HFT domain, this capability is improved by being able to react to market data more quickly than other participants can. Other forms of so-called technical analysis, such as statistical arbitrage, enable HFTs to use predefined statistical models of securities to detect situations where the price seems to be out of line with its expected value, enabling an arbitrage opportunity. Again, being able to get in and out of a position quickly, made possible in part by fast computers and low latency to the market system, can produce small profits that add up over time. Latency itself can become equivalent to profit in other strategies whereby an algorithm discovers a price discrepancy between the same security available on multiple ECNs, that is, one traded on, say, both BATS and the NASDAQ.[16] More esoteric and, from the point of view of some participants, problematic strategies come under what has been termed the "darker arts." For example, *stuffing* is when a HFT algorithm submits more orders to the market than the market can handle, potentially causing problems for so-called slower traders. *Smoking* involves submitting orders that are initially attractive to slower traders that are quickly changed to less generous terms, whereas *spoofing* is when, for example, a HFT algorithm posts orders to sell, when the actual intent is to buy.[17]

16. For more on these strategies, see Gomber et al., "High-Frequency Trading," 24–31.

17. Bruno Biais and Paul Woolley, "High Frequency Trading," preliminary paper (2011), 8–9. The recent Dodd-Frank act to "overhaul" the financial system in the wake of the crisis would seem to outlaw the practice of spoofing; see Silla Brush and Asjylyn Loder, "CFTC Told Disruptive

It has become clear, however, that even if HFT algorithms are staying on the legal side of what is permissible, there are still major concerns regarding fairness, especially as it relates to quote availability. Nanex LLC, one of the firms most active in critiquing HFT, has shown that a large percentage of quotes for securities are canceled within milliseconds, preventing these quotes from reaching the West Coast of the United States.[18] This is one of the most important pieces of evidence regarding the acceleration of HFT and contemporary finance, as it indexes a speed far beyond the capability of a day trader or even an institutional investor. The capital required to perform at these speeds ensures that the best quotes will only exist for those with the vast sums available to invest in this computational infrastructure, creating a vastly uneven playing field.

Although we now know much more about HFT than we used to, for many years it indeed was a "dark" practice, both in the sense of the shadow that hid open discussion of these techniques and in its obscurity to the general public. All that changed on May 6, 2010, the day of what became known as the Flash Crash and the main reason for my exposition of AT and HFT. The full details of this day are beyond the scope of this essay, so I will only outline them schematically, following the findings of the official U.S. report produced by the CFTC and the SEC,[19] although recent developments have cast doubt on

---

Trading Rules Threaten Market Liquidity," December 2, 2010, http://www.bloomberg.com/news/2010-12-02/commodities-regulators-told-disruptive-trading-rules-threaten-liquidity.html. However, in practice, it is very difficult actually to detect this activity.

18. Eric Scott Hunsader, "What's Wrong with the Stock Market? Here Mr. Berman, This Is Fraud (Made from SEC Data)," February 11, 2015, https://twitter.com/nanexllc/status/565525073885663232.

19. Commodity Futures Trading Commission and U.S. Securities and Exchange Commission, "Findings Regarding the Market Events of

the official story.[20] In short, between the hours of 2:00 and 3:00 P.M. Eastern time, the NYSE had its largest single-day loss up to that day, a loss of nearly one thousand points, with a subsequent rebound that resulted in the second largest intraday swing up to then. The actual dynamics of the event were difficult to reconstruct after the fact, but it would appear that a single large sell-off (to the order of $4.1 billion) of a particular index security, the E-Mini S&P, caused a cascade of trading activity by HFT algorithms using many of the techniques just described. This initial trade was, in retrospect, due to a relatively poor choice of a given AT that did not take into account its own potential impact on the market. Activity by various HFT algorithms responding to this trade resulted in the buying and selling of more than twenty-seven thousand E-Mini S&P contracts with a net change of only two hundred points. Although built-in trading pauses occurred because of the activity on the E-Mini S&P, liquidity still evaporated as time passed, causing share prices on some stocks to go to extremes, such as a penny or $100,000, which were the computational limits on prices on

---

May 6th, 2010," report of the Staffs of the CFTC and SEC to the Joint Advisory Committee Emerging Regulatory Issues, September 30, 2010.

20. Criminal charges have been brought against a British trader, Navinder Singh Sarao, in connection with his alleged manipulation of the market prior to, and on the day of, the Flash Crash. While governmental prosecutors claim that this arrest is proof of their hard line against market manipulation, others believe that Sarao is merely a scapegoat for more systemic issues that I highlight later. See Nathaniel Popper and Jenny Anderson, "Trader Arrested in Manipulation That Contributed to 2010 'Flash Crash,'" *New York Times,* April 21, 2015, http://www.nytimes.com/2015/04/22/business/dealbook/trader-in-britain-arrested-on-charges-of-manipulation-that-led-to-2010-flash-crash.html; Rajiv Sethi, "The Trader as Scapegoat," *New York Times,* April 28, 2015, http://mobile.nytimes.com/2015/04/28/opinion/the-trader-as-scapegoat.html.

these exchanges. Even so, the pauses in trading enabled the same algorithms and participants to buy up seemingly erroneously priced securities, leading to the trade of more than 2 billion shares over a twenty minute period and the recovery of the market.[21]

Speculation around the cause(s) of the Flash Crash began immediately, with much of the blame directed at HFT. Although the report of the CFTC and the SEC did not lay blame on HFT in particular, it did indicate how HFT algorithms contributed to the large price swings, the immense number of shares traded, and the drying up of liquidity.[22] Trying to work out the exact dynamics of the Flash Crash has become popular, but determinations are made difficult by a number of factors. First, because trading on these exchanges is done relatively anonymously, there is no way to gather, after the fact, the distribution of trades due to all of the participating firms. Second, and as a result, reconstructions of the event must rely on a number of assumptions of what exactly constitutes HFT and which sets of trades might be due to individual participants. Nevertheless, most of the postmortems—as well as studies published prior to the Flash Crash—affirm relatively positive contributions of HFT algorithms to the markets, specifically in their ability to provide liquidity—the very thing that evaporated during the Flash Crash.[23] In short, the consensus among most financial

21. For another take on the sequence of these events, see MacKenzie, "How to Make Money in Microseconds."

22. Commodity Futures Trading Commission and U.S. Securities and Exchange Commission, "Findings Regarding the Market Events of May 6th, 2010," 1–8.

23. See, e.g., David Easley, Marcos M. López De Prado, and Maureen O'Hara, "The Microstructure of the 'Flash Crash': Flow Toxicity, Liquidity Crashes, and the Probability of Informed Trading," *Journal of Portfolio Management* 37, no. 2 (2011): 118–28; Gomber et al., "High-Frequency

economists is that the Flash Crash was a particularly extreme event and that HFT does not in general increase volatility in the market, and thus HFT ultimately improves the "efficiency" of the market.[24] Some, however, are beginning to have reservations. A recent article in the *New York Times* written after another AT meltdown notes the following:

> Terrence Hendershott, a professor at the University of California, Berkeley, said he had been an advocate for technological innovation in the past, but had begun to wonder if the continuing battle for technological superiority had become too much.
>
> "You've got arguably too many people, in too small a space, and they just keep spending enormous amounts of money," Professor Hendershott said. "Can I convince myself that we are really seeing a lot of benefits? No."[25]

What is clear is that HFT, along with other changes in the market as a result of different behaviors by humans and machines,

---

Trading"; Joel Hasbrouck and Gideon Saar, "Low-Latency Trading," Johnson School Research Paper Series 35-2010, 2011; Andrei Kirilenko et al., "The Flash Crash: The Impact of High Frequency Trading on an Electronic Market," working paper, 2011.

24. Foresight Project, "The Future of Computer Trading in Financial Markets," working paper, U.K. government Office for Science, 2011, 9–12. A contrary perspective can be found in Frank Zhang, "High-Frequency Trading, Stock Volatility, and Price Discovery," 2010, http://papers.ssrn.com/sol3/papers.cfm?abstract_id=1691679. Zhang's result is dismissed by the authors of the Foresight report on methodological grounds.

25. Nathaniel Popper, "On Wall Street, the Rising Cost of Faster Trades," *New York Times,* August 13, 2012, https://www.nytimes.com/2012/08/14/business/on-wall-street-the-rising-cost-of-high-speed-trading.html. For Hendershott's previous positions, see Terrence Hendershott, Charles M. Jones, and Albert J. Menkveld, "Does Algorithmic Trading Improve Liquidity?," *Journal of Finance* 66, no. 1 (2011): 1–33; Terrence Hendershott and Ryan Riodan, "Algorithmic Trading and Information," NET Institute Working Paper 09-08, 2011.

as well as regulatory pressures pushing for more competition, has made the markets more interconnected, leading to definite challenges for the authorities in assigning clear blame. Recent studies commissioned by the U.K. government suggest that it therefore might be necessary to understand markets today within an "ultra large-scale system of systems"—similar to nuclear power plants or highly complex technical artifacts such as the Space Shuttle—that requires appropriate modeling or an "ecology of practices" that would recognize multiple market equilibria with multiple paths toward efficiency.[26]

If HFT were only important in situations such as the Flash Crash, then it might be considered simply a contributing factor to so-called black swan events, events whose probability is extremely low yet not nonzero.[27] However, it is estimated that HFT is responsible for anywhere between 40 and 70 percent of all trading volume in the United States, 35 and 40 percent of trading volume in Europe, and slightly less in Canada, although it is difficult to know how these percentages are determined.[28] Given that HFT seems to contribute to volatility of the market, and that HFT strategies depend on taking advantage of minuscule, millisecond-level changes in price, it behooves us to ask how a concept of noise might contribute to our understanding of the phenomena. A recent paper by Frank J. Fabozzi, Sergio M. Focardi, and Caroline Jonas draws from a concept from econometrics known as microstructure noise to help explain the ac-

26. Dave Cliff and Linda Northrop, "The Global Financial Markets: An Ultra-Large-Scale Systems Perspective," *Future of Computer Trading in Financial Markets—Foresight Driver Review* DR 4 (2010); Farmer and Skouras, "An Ecological Perspective."

27. Nassim Nicholas Taleb, *The Black Swan: The Impact of the Highly Improbable* (New York: Random House, 2007).

28. Fabozzi et al., "High-Frequency Trading," 8.

tivity of HFT and what they term high-frequency data (HFD), HFT's necessary counterpart. A definition of microstructure noise is difficult to pin down, but one quant suggests two important distinctions: first, to an economist, microstructure noise is whatever makes it difficult to estimate the value of some particular time series of data; second, to market participants, microstructure noise is whatever causes observed values to deviate from the "fundamentals."[29] I am interested in this second aspect of microstructure noise, as it is precisely this assumed *deviation* that enables HFT to work as well as what could connect HFT to the earlier discussion of noise traders.

Fabozzi, Focardi, and Jonas's paper is one of the few to pay attention to the role of noise within HFT. Their study is both a meta-review of other papers investigating HFT and a series of interviews with market participants themselves. Importantly, their interviews show the role that *infrastructure* plays in constructing and propagating this noise. Information received from the exchanges must go through a process of "cleansing" to remove "erroneous data"; similarly, the amount of noise within a sample will depend on the exchange it came from and the types of securities being traded there.[30] More fundamentally, noise would seem to be the corruption of what is assumed to be an ideally perfectly observable process. As indicated by this section's epigraph, noise is for some researchers simply a "mathematical idealization" that, through its removal in their models, enables one to provide a better measure of the "true" nature of the process.

Yet for others, microstructure noise does have an independent existence from the mathematics that make it necessary.

29. Palace Chan, "Statistics—What Exactly Is Meant by 'Microstructure Noise'?," November 11, 2011, http://quant.stackexchange .com/questions/2360/what-exactly-is-meant-by-microstructure-noise.

30. Fabozzi et al., "High-Frequency Trading," 11, 19.

Consider, for example, the comments of Ravi Jagannathan, codirector of the Financial Institutions and Markets Research Center at Northwestern University:

> If markets are frictionless, that is, if there are no microstructure effects, the higher the frequency, the better the measurement of values as volatility. However, in rare or severe events, HFD are of no help; microstructure—the way people trade, the strategies used, lack of knowledge of what the others are doing—becomes more important.[31]

Microstructure noise becomes a necessary deviation as a result of human activity, of interconnected systems, of processes that do not perfectly follow mathematical idealizations. Whereas it would seem from this quotation that Jagannathan understands microstructure noise as occurring only at the level of the rare event—such as the Flash Crash—others are beginning to understand this noise as a continual component of the market. Frederi Viens, professor of mathematics and statistics at Purdue University, says, "My guess is that microstructure noise is real, so that we simply have to deal with it, that is to say, account for the added uncertainty in our prices."[32] At a more stark level, Nikolaus Hautsch of Humboldt University observes,

> HFD are affected by a lot of noise, lots of data with no information content. What matters is the ratio between the signal to noise. The signal-to-noise ratio must be greater than 1. If not, we have more noise than signal, and no gain. In the very beginning, the role of noise was overlooked. Over the past four, five years, we have gained a better understanding of this.[33]

31. Ravi Jagannathan, quoted in ibid., 16.
32. Frederi Viens, quoted in ibid., 17.
33. Nikolaus Hautsch, quoted in ibid., 18.

Nevertheless, for Hautsch, noise becomes reinscribed within standard information theory as the dual of signal, of something to be removed, something lacking in "information content." Microstructure noise, in the accounts of both Hautsch and Viens, is a continual component of the market yet remains an impediment to ever more precise estimates of the "actual" price.

Other expressions of noise, beyond the narrowly informatic, have also come about as a result of the Flash Crash; these noises interfere with the attempt to cleave noise from signal. Recall from the previous section my discussion of squawk boxes, audio feeds from the open-outcry pits, and, specifically, the services provided by companies such as Traders Audio. On the day of the Flash Crash, these feeds were of course live, resulting in recordings of the sounds from the pits during the event. Ben Lichenstein of Traders Audio has become somewhat of a minor celebrity on financial blogs because of his reporting that day; a recording of his reporting is available for download from blogs such as *Zero Hedge*.[34] Listening to this recording is a disorienting experience, not least because of the problem of the specialized terminology of the pits. More important is the affect, the *tone,* of Lichenstein's voice as the recording goes on. He begins in what I would characterize as an incredulous voice, questioning the very trades that he can see and hear before him. But shortly this shifts into pure anxiety and fear, the gravel in his voice bouncing from lows to highs in pitch. Though the microphone is clearly directed at him, the shouts and cries from

34. Tyler Durden, "MUST HEAR: Panic and Loathing from the S&P 500 Pits," *Zero Hedge* (blog), May 7, 2010, http://www.zerohedge.com/article/panic-and-loathing-sp-500-pits. *Zero Hedge* is a group blog with most posts signed anonymously by "Tyler Durden," a character from the novel *Fight Club*.

the pits can be heard in the background. Heavy breathing fills what would normally be heard as pauses. The intensity of the volume—perhaps a mirror of the volume of the securities—is distorted by what sounds like a poor-quality microphone. In short, the archive of Lichenstein's reporting produces a bodily trace of the anxiety of that day, one that cannot be captured by the plethora of graphs, tables, and commentary produced in response to the event. It is a trace that, again, we can accept as affectual because of the ultimate effects of the financial crisis.

A different yet just as entrancing marker of that day comes from the French artist collective rybn. For a number of years, their work has explored the concept of "antidatamining," that is, use of the data-mining techniques of computational capitalism to shed light on the intersection of data and society.[35] One of their recent exhibited works, *ADM8,* is an automated "trading bot performance" that uses AT to predict price movements in stocks to capture profit. The performance is meant to end if the bot becomes bankrupt, but as of the time of writing, it had a net profit of €1,475 since August 2011.[36] Yet it is an earlier work I want to listen to, namely, their direct response to the Flash Crash called *FLASHCRASH SONIFICATION.*[37] Sonification—the translation into sound of data collected for nonsonic purposes—is a well-known practice within experimental music and is being taken up in the sciences.[38] For

35. rybn, "ANTIDATAMINING," n.d., http://www.antidatamining.net/.

36. rybn, "ANTIDATAMINING VIII," February 9, 2015, http://rybn.org/ANTI/ADM8/.

37. rybn, "FLASHCRASH SONIFICATION," n.d., http://rybn.free.fr/ANTI/FLASHCRASH.html.

38. Alexandra Supper, "The Search for the 'Killer Application': Drawing the Boundaries around the Sonification of Scientific Data," in *Oxford Handbook of Science Studies,* ed. Trevor Pinch and Karen Bijsterveld,

FLASHCRASH SONIFICATION, rybn took trading data from nine different exchanges on the afternoon of the Flash Crash and created an austere, digitally sharp, yet undulating soundscape that recalls the work of Ryoji Ikeda or Carsten Nicolai, but without their rhythmic precision. The data rybn used came from the market data firm Nanex.[39] It's important to listen to their online-available, two-channel mix on headphones to appreciate the details of the piece. Beginning with a loud uncorrelated noise, the piece quickly becomes quiet, punctuated in a seemingly random fashion with high-frequency bursts. About six minutes in, a ghostly wave of mid-frequency noise starts to wobble, joined by lower-frequency rumbling. Four minutes from the end, the high-frequency pulses become louder and more rhythmic, sounding as if the spaces between them were slowing decreasing. A few seconds before the sonification ends, the pulses rapidly start to smear together until they merge into a continuous sound, thereby ending the piece.

The collective rybn constructed the piece specifically for the installation environment, a planetarium, at Le Lieu Multiple in Poitiers, France, for an exhibition in spring 2011 titled *Raison d'Agir.* The two-channel version is a mixdown of the complete nine channels presented in this space, in which the sounds from eight different exchanges surrounded the sonification of the NYSE in the middle. While the recording is somewhat quiet, the live version was louder, not so much to recall noise musical acts, such as Merzbow, as to emphasize the intensity of the bass levels. The building toward the end of the piece was

---

249–70 (Oxford: Oxford University Press, 2011).

39. The data are available from http://www.nanex.net/20100506 /FlashCrashAnalysis_Intro.html. Free access to this kind of detailed data is rare and thus, absent Nanex's posting of it online, the sonification would have been expensive and perhaps impossible to produce.

meant to "emphasize the moment of the crash, [by] adding an effect of resonance, which propagates slowly, making it more tense, as the krach goes on."[40] Thus, instead of merely transparently translating the data into sound, rybn constructed the sonification to bring out this resonance: "resonance is pointed [to] as one of the major risk[s] of HFT by many economists and the feedback phenomenon was in the center of our discussions when we were preparing the piece." Isolating the Flash Crash was important for rybn, as it was perhaps the "moment when people started to understand financ[ial] orientations more clearly," thereby highlighting the symptomatic nature of the "speculative short-term loop finance seems to be stuck in."

Noise thus works here via multiple interfering fields. There is on the surface the resonance with various strands of noise music and contemporary sonic practice that take any form of data and transform them into sound. But there is informatic noise in the digital signal as well, a trace that we encountered earlier as microstructure noise. In rybn's view, this is because "HFT brings in more confusion and chaos (in mathematical terms)." This is not something "natural," however: "the whole signal remains fabricated, and is based on very complex phenomen[a] of feedback interactions. . . . Financial noise is created by the sum of all its internal feedbacks, anticipation process[es], and mimetic forces. The noise we can produce in the framework of antidatamining, is based on the matter we explore. HFT provides a wide range of frequencies, infinite structural composition sets, and a strong symbolic and metaphoric matter." Noise is to be found in this materiality of data, the same material that is located in places such as the

40. Quotations in this and the following paragraph come from rybn, e-mail interview with the author, April 27, 2012.

NYSE's data center, the same material that can be translated into pressure waves in the air.

Paired with the sonification on rybn's website is a "natal chart" of the stock market that suggests that the divination of prices can be done through the consultation of astrological charts. This is a clear comment on contemporary financial discourse, as rybn argues that "news and media try to interpret the obscure behavior of 'the markets' as in the ancient practising of Haruspicy," or divination through the entrails of sacrificed animals, with the image meant as "an attempt to criticize the degree of mysticism that finance has reached."

While not explicitly intended by rybn, *FLASHCRASH SONIFICATION* also recalls *Black Shoals Stock Market Planetarium* (2002–4) by Lise Autogena, Joshua Portway, Cefn Hoile, and Tom Riley, an installation consisting of an overhead projection of stock market data in the form of constellations that are constantly changing due to the calculations of artificial-life creatures who "feed" on the joint market activity of related companies.[41] While the name of the piece references the Black–Scholes–Merton equation discussed earlier, the project itself is about stock market valuations and not derivatives per se. *Black Shoals* has garnered much critical attention in subsequent years, specifically in its attempt to understand the constructed nature of the financial system via the feedback dynamics of its alife creatures.[42] However, I think it is important to delineate the ways in which *FLASHCRASH SONIFICATION*

41. Lise Autogena and Joshua Portway, *Black Shoals Stock Market Planetarium*, catalog published in conjunction with the exhibition from February 6 to April 12, 2004, Copenhagen Contemporary Art Center.

42. Brian Holmes, "Is it Written in the Stars? Global Finance, Precarious Destinies," *ephemera: theory and politics in organization* 10, nos. 3–4 (2010): 222–33.

differs from *Black Shoals,* specifically with respect to funding and support. Lise Autogena notes that *Black Shoals* raised approximately £70,000 and required special agreements from Reuters for access to its data feed and to the "sensitive closed data handling systems" of the Copenhagen Stock Exchange.[43] *FLASHCRASH SONIFICATION,* conversely, is of a piece with rybn's practice of using publicly available financial data, either published by corporations such as Nanex, as in *FLASHCRASH SONIFICATION,* or scraped from sites such as Yahoo! Finance with repeated requests masked by IP proxies.[44] Access to market data is big business, and thus it is important to ask in what ways a project like *Black Shoals,* with its necessary interrelationships with major market producers, can function as a critical intervention, no matter the sophistication of its "allegory of the trader's condition," in the words of Brian Holmes.[45]

Additionally, I disagree with Rita Raley's interpretation of *Black Shoals,* specifically her contention that it is a "socially engaged, participatory, and pedagogical intervention into the discourse on financial markets."[46] More so, the rhetoric of *Black Shoals*'s generative techniques sits comfortably close to that of Hayek discussed earlier; in the words of *Black Shoals*'s artificial-life programmer Cefn Hoile, the "organisms" are produced by a "decentralised evolutionary process—a result of limited resource availability combined with co-evolutionary interactions"—in other words, via processes that are similar to

43. Lise Autogena, "Lise Autogena," n.d., http://research.ncl.ac.uk/sacs/projects/Autogena4.html.

44. An exception to this is *ADM8,* discussed previously, as it required direct access to the market to execute the trades.

45. Holmes, "Is It Written in the Stars?," 224.

46. Rita Raley, *Tactical Media* (Minneapolis: University of Minnesota Press, 2009), 149.

those of Hayek's market.[47] This is perhaps only a parallel tendency, in line with a particular zeitgeist associated with alife research at the turn of the most recent century; nevertheless, the historical antecedents of this within economic thought need to be noted. To do so might enable us to question whether the insight Raley draws from *Black Shoals* ("we are always caught within a paradigm that is too complex and that in effect manages us") is all that we can hope for within art that engages with financial markets.[48]

FLASHCRASH SONIFICATION is a layered comment on this state of affairs: a direct critique of the obscurantism of contemporary financial language; a foregrounding of the ways in which sacrificial, seemingly "wasteful" loss of value is translated into meaningful discursive signs; and a noisy environment that pulls human perception into the time frame of algorithms. In *FLASHCRASH SONIFICATION,* sonic noise becomes a translation of the data from the market—abstract yet eminently material—into a different abstract form that does not immediately signify. Like the recording of Lichenstein from the pits, *FLASHCRASH SONIFICATION* suggests rather than indicates. Listening to it cannot provide us with rational information regarding the dynamics of the Flash Crash; instead, it produces a dark foreboding of the mechanisms at work, the high-frequency pulses first recalling heartbeats that soon speed up beyond any ability for distinction. This darkness is heightened through what Steve Goodman might term "bass materialism," or the tactility of the sub-bass levels that are coupled to the increasing speed of the higher pulses at the end of the

47. Cefn Hoile, *Black Shoals: Evolving Organisms in a World of Financial Data,* n.d. 1.

48. Raley, *Tactical Media,* 149.

piece.[49] *FLASHCRASH SONIFICATION* is slightly off-kilter yet still analogous to genres of precisely ordered electronic music, and thus comments on the inability for computation—and, by extension, the market—to be the perfectly rational, ordered space it is ideally understood to be.

49. Steve Goodman, *Sonic Warfare: Sound, Affect, and the Ecology of Fear* (Cambridge, Mass.: MIT Press, 2009), 196. It should go without saying that this is a pun on Georges Bataille's notion of "base materialism."

Noisy Accelerationism

Photonic Hypercapital digitizes eschatology.

—CCRU[1]

IT SHOULD BE CLEAR NOW HOW NOISE MATTERS TO FINANCE. Noise is the dual of information; yet people trading on noise can sometimes make more money and last longer in the market than those trading on information. Noise works to upend models of efficient markets. Noise as sound can indicate potential trading opportunities as well as being indispensable to the smooth functioning of the market. Noise as volatility or fluctuation as time approaches zero is a means for the continual accumulation of small profits. The intersection of informatic and sonic noise produces, on one hand, vocal indications of fear and panic and, on the other, a dark, ghostly cloud from the onslaught of data. How do we understand these interferences, these contradic-

1. Ccru, "Swarmachines," n.d., http://www.ccru.net/swarm1/1_swarm.htm.

tions that seem to exceed our existing frameworks? The ways in which we respond to this materiality of noise in flesh and machines will help construct our methodologies for addressing the imbrication of finance and contemporary life and might also tell us something about how to deal with the complexity of humans and machines.

The acceleration discussed in the previous chapter—indexed perhaps most dramatically by the fact that Einstein's theory of special relativity is now a valid reference point for finance—provides one suggestion. But an acceleration toward *what*? In a historical materialist account, to reach a point where communism—or some other form of social relationship not mediated by the commodity form—can become possible, capitalism must first become extinct. Highlighting and exploiting the internal contradictions of capitalism then becomes one key part of the revolutionary project, of the process of dialectical materialism. Such contradictions are highlighted during most leftist protests these days, and the recent climate marches in New York City in September 2014 were no exception. The day after tens of thousands marched through midtown New York in support of global action against climate change, there was a massive protest titled Flood Wall Street that attempted to march to the NYSE. Police not only prevented activists from getting to the stock exchange but also protected the iconic bull nearby with their presence and crowd-control fencing. The attention to the bull's safety is a curious spectacle, as it implies that it is the bull *itself* that is the locus of modern finance. But we know that this is not the case. What might have been the power of the protests—and, importantly, the spectacle *surrounding* the protests—if they had left the bull alone and instead traveled to 1700 MacArthur Boulevard in Mahwah, New Jersey?

Such a choice is only possible if one understands that the real physical manifestation of the market is among the whirring computers and air-conditioning units rather than people on the floor of the hallowed NYSE. But if critiquing this protest is not heresy enough, what if we wanted to push things further? To not just remain in the realm of critique but rather to suggest that we need to *accelerate* the processes that produced HFT in the first place? Perhaps such an acceleration could bring capitalism to its foreseen end in less time. And what if that acceleration could use the very mechanisms of capitalism itself?

Such a tendency, latent within Marxist thought over the past century and a half, has only recently been given a name, in a derogatory sense, by the British philosopher Benjamin Noys: *accelerationism.*[2] More recently, Steven Shaviro has outlined some of the various strands of accelerationism in his *No Speed Limit: Three Essays on Accelerationism.*[3] Drawing on an intellectual lineage that begins most recently with the early 1970s work of Gilles Deleuze and Félix Guattari and Jean-François Lyotard, that resurfaces in the 1990s with the theory-fiction of Nick Land, and that was resurrected during the most recent financial crisis, accelerationism is a theorization of the conditions and techniques for the hastening of the contradictions of capitalism to produce its ultimate downfall. Such techniques are predicated on a fundamentally antihumanistic position, one that is weakly reflective of similar recent approaches, for example, in actor-network theory or object-oriented ontology, but that radically explodes their implications.[4]

2. Benjamin Noys, "Accelerationism," *No Useless Leniency* (blog), October 20, 2008, http://leniency.blogspot.com/2008/10/accelerationism.html.

3. Steven Shaviro, *No Speed Limit: Three Essays on Accelerationism,* Forerunners: Ideas First (Minneapolis: University of Minnesota Press, 2015).

4. Most dramatic, of course, is Marx's contention, in the "Fragment on Machines" of the *Grundrisse,* that humans will merely become the

Accelerationist reference points come from the early Deleuze and Guattari of *Anti-Oedipus* and the early Lyotard of *Libidinal Economy*. For Deleuze and Guattari, the central conceit is the schizophrenia of capitalism: while it requires the reterritorialization of flows to capture surplus value and reinscribe the logic of Oedipus, it must simultaneously produce their deterritorialization to unleash desire: "Capitalism tends toward a threshold of decoding that will destroy the socius in order to make it a body without organs and unleash the flows of desire on this body as a deterritorialized field."[5] In this interference of de- and reterritorialization, what is to be done? Writing from within the conflicts of the early 1970s over the relationship of the Communist Party to new social movements, the solution for Deleuze and Guattari was eminently *not* to be found within the formulations of Party politics. Rather, Deleuze and Guattari suggested that perhaps deterritorialization was not being pushed far enough:

> But which is the revolutionary path? Is there one?—To withdraw from the world market, as Samir Amin advises Third World countries to do, in a curious revival of the fascist "economic solution"? Or might it be to go in the opposite direction? To go still further, that is, in the movement of the market, of decoding and deterritorialization? For perhaps the flows are not yet deterritorialized enough, not decoded enough, from the viewpoint of a theory and a practice of a highly schizophrenic character. Not to withdraw from the process, but to go further, to "accelerate the process," as Nietzsche put it: in this matter, the truth is that we haven't seen anything yet.[6]

"conscious linkages" of machines. See Karl Marx, *Grundrisse: Foundations of the Critique of Political Economy,* trans. Martin Nicolaus (1939; repr., London: Penguin Classics, 1973), 690–712.

    5. Gilles Deleuze and Félix Guattari, *Anti-Oedipus: Capitalism and Schizophrenia,* trans. Robert Hurley, Mark Seem, and Helen R. Lane (1972; repr., Minneapolis: University of Minnesota Press, 1983), 33.

    6. Ibid., 239–40.

But this ceaseless directionality toward ever more deterritorialized flows is tempered in *A Thousand Plateaus*:

> You have to keep enough of the organism for it to reform each dawn; and you have to keep small supplies of significance and subjectification, if only to turn them against their own systems when the circumstances demand it, when things, persons, even situations, force you to; and you have to keep small rations of subjectivity in sufficient quantity to enable you to respond to the dominant reality. Mimic the strata. You don't reach the BwO [Body without Organs], and its plane of consistency, by wildly destratifying.[7]

"When the circumstances demand it," "mimic the strata"— these are not the phrases of an acceleration toward ultimate deterritorialization but rather a statement of pragmatics in the dawning years of Reagan-Thatcher neoliberalism. And even in *Anti-Oedipus,* they noted that "No one has ever died from contradictions".[8]

Lyotard published *Libidinal Economy* shortly after, and partially in response to, *Anti-Oedipus*; he would later refer to it as his "evil book," and evidently it caused much trouble between him and his former Marxist colleagues and comrades from his time in *Socialisme ou Barbarie.*[9] If possible, Lyotard's evocations of desire are more intense than those of Deleuze and Guattari in *Anti-Oedipus*; as writing becomes intensity, libidinality does not merely remain as potential: "Our danger, we libidinal econ-

7. Gilles Deleuze and Félix Guattari, *A Thousand Plateaus: Capitalism and Schizophrenia,* trans. Brian Massumi (1980; repr., Minneapolis: University of Minnesota Press, 1987), 160.

8. Deleuze and Guattari, *Anti-Oedipus,* 151.

9. Lyotard, quoted in Iain Hamilton Grant, introduction to *Libidinal Economy,* trans. Iain Hamilton Grant (Bloomington: Indiana University Press, 1993), xviii.

omists, lies in building a new morality with this consolation, of proclaiming and broadcasting that the libidinal band *is good,* that the circulation of affects *is joyful,* that the anonymity and the incompossibilty of figures *are great and free,* that all pain is reactionary and conceals the points of a formation issuing from the great Zero."[10] The "circulation of affects" is already to be found within the bodily practices of the proletariat; here Lyotard deserves to be quoted at length:

> Why, political intellectuals, do you *incline towards* the proletariat? In commiseration for what? I realize that a proletarian would hate you, you have no hatred because you are bourgeois, privileged smooth-skinned types, but also because you dare not say the only important thing there is to say, that one can enjoy swallowing the shit of capital, its materials, its metal bars, its polystyrene, its books, its sausage pâtés, swallowing tonnes of it till you burst—and because instead of saying this, which is *also* what happens in the desire of those who work with their hands, arses and heads, ah, you become a leader of *men,* what a leader of *pimps,* you lean forward and divulge: ah, but that's alienation, it isn't pretty, hang on, we'll save you from it, we will work to liberate you from this wicked affection for servitude, we will give you dignity. And in this way you situate yourselves on the most despicable side, the moralistic side where you desire that our capitalized's desire be totally ignored, forbidden, brought to a standstill, you are like priests with sinners, our servile intensities frighten you, you have to tell yourselves: how they must suffer to endure that! And of course we suffer, we the capitalized, but this does not mean that we do not enjoy, nor that what you think you can offer us as a remedy—for what?—does not disgust us, even more. We abhor therapeutics and its vaseline, we prefer to burst under the quantitative excesses that you judge the most stupid. And don't wait for our spontaneity to rise up in revolt either.[11]

10. Lyotard, *Libidinal Economy,* 11, emphasis original.
11. Ibid., 115–16, emphasis original.

Lyotard's vitriol is directed against those who would postpone revolution (the Party), postpone desire (the reterritorialization of Capital, in the language of Deleuze and Guattari), and postpone the enjoyment of the proletariat (the "political intellectuals"). In Lyotard's view, this postponement needs to be burst open: "We desire the effects of conduction and the conduction of effects. Lysis, thesis."[12] Although *Libidinal Economy* has been excoriated for this passage in particular, I think it is too hasty to deny the fundamental claim Lyotard makes here, namely, that there might be some sort of enjoyment in the actions of capitalistic machines on the body; we can accept this point while simultaneously suggesting that something needs to be done regarding the physical damage that occurs. For subjugation is not simply a negative experience, as the practices of sadomasochism show, but rather a complicated conjugation of humans, machines, and practices that should not be dismissed so quickly.

Noys notes that for Deleuze and Guattari (as we can understand from certain passages in *A Thousand Plateaus*) as well as for Lyotard (as evidenced in some texts from the 1980s and early 1990s), the move toward a slowing down of the unleashing of desire might have reflected the realization that their earlier positions were becoming "congruent with capitalist flows."[13] Yet these trajectories were soon to have another adherent within the work of the renegade academic Nick Land and his colleagues and students at the Cybernetic Culture Research Unit (Ccru) at the University of Warwick in the mid-1990s. Among the hype of the potentials of the Internet and its professed ability to deterritorialize all traditional categories—race, ethnicity,

12. Ibid., 259.

13. Benjamin Noys, *The Persistence of the Negative: A Critique of Contemporary Continental Theory* (Edinburgh: Edinburgh University Press, 2010), 8.

gender, class, humanism—Land, along with the codirector of the Ccru, Sadie Plant, produced a number of visceral texts and performances that reactivated the accelerationist tendencies of the earlier works by Deleuze, Guattari, and Lyotard.[14] Land's dynamical evocations are a reworked invocation of Nietzsche, Kant, Bataille, computational technology, viruses, drugs, and what he and Sadie Plant term the "cyberpositive." Recalling Norbert Wiener's valorization of negative over positive feedback, Plant and Land write that

> the modern Human Security System might even have appeared with Wiener's subliminal insight that everything cyberpositive is an enemy of mankind. Evolving out of work on weaponry guidance systems, his was an attempt to enslave cybernetics to a general defence technology against alien invasion. Cybernetics was itself to be kept under control, under a control that was not itself cybernetic. It is as if his thinking were guided by a blind tropism of evasion, away from another, deeper, runaway process: from a technics losing control and a communication with the outside of man.[15]

Whereas Wiener understood the negative feedback of cybernetics as enacting a stabilizing force on systems, a position

14. For one of the few in-depth articles on the Ccru, see Simon Reynolds 1999 article "Renegade Academia: The Cybernetic Culture Research Unit," *Energy Flash* (blog), November 3, 2009, http://energyflashbysimonreynolds. blogspot.com/2009/11/renegade-academia-cybernetic-culture.html. Besides Land and Plant, the Ccru also included, at various points, many writers, artists, and musicians who are well known today: Steve Goodman, Kodwo Eshun, Luciana Parisi, Robin MacKay, and Mark Fischer, among others.

15. Sadie Plant and Nick Land, "Cyberpositive," in *Unnatural: Techno-Theory for a Contaminated Culture,* ed. Matthew Fuller (London: Underground, 1994), n.p. This text is also available online; see http:// www.sterneck.net/cyber/plant-land-cyber/index.php.

that resonates with his fundamental humanism that was key to his later writings, Plant and Land, following in the waves unleashed by Deleuze, Guattari, and Lyotard, moved to the other end of the binary, provocatively suggesting that positive feedback, though uncontrollable in principle, could in fact enable a certain antihumanism, one that would allow for the "communication with the outside of man."

Land released the cyberpositive in delirious works of theory-fiction that, depending on one's taste, are either the highlight or the doldrums of 1990s cultural theory. Land's texts, long available only in obscure journals that have long gone out of print, were recently published in an edited collection of his work, the release of which was the occasion for a symposium in 2010 around this question of accelerationism. It is here that we can reconnect to the questions of noise and finance that have been the topic of this essay. Consider the following quotation regarding the potential of finance capital from his 1993 article "Machinic Desire":

> The obsolete psychological category of "greed" privatizes and moralizes addiction, as if the profit-seeking tropism of a transnational capitalism propagating itself through epidemic consumerism were intelligible in terms of personal subjective traits. Wanting more is the index of interlock with cyberpositive machinic processes, and not the expression of private idiosyncrasy. What could be more impersonal—disinterested—than a haut bourgeois capital expansion servo-mechanism striving to double $10 billion? And even these creatures are disappearing into silicon viro-finance automatisms, where massively distributed and anonymized human ownership has become as vacuously nominal as democratic sovereignty. . . .
>
> Markets are part of the infrastructure—its immanent intelligence—and thus entirely indissociable from the forces of production. It makes no more sense to try to rescue the economy from capital by demarketization than it does to liberate the prole-

tarian from false consciousness by decortication. In neither case would one be left with anything except a radically dysfunctional wreck, terminally shut-down hardware.[16]

Land evokes Lyotard's contempt for those who would "speak" for the proletariat while graphically noting the embeddedness of capital markets within society; the removal of markets would leave nothing but a "dysfunctional wreck." Latent within these passages, as well as others in the text, is a foreboding tone toward the potential for transformation that removes accelerationism from the realm of choice. This is perhaps most evident in a later text from 1995 titled "No Future":

> Mass computer commoditization de-differentiates consumption and investment, triggering cultural micro-engineering waves that dissociate theopolitical action into machinic hybridities, amongst increasingly dysfunctional defensive convulsions. Acephalization = schizophrenia: cutting-up capital by way of bottom-up macrobacterial telecommerce, inducing corporate disintegration. The doomed part of intensively virtualized techonomic apparatuses subverts the fraying residues of anthropomorphic guidance. Control dissolves into the impossible.[17]

This lack of control, this orientation toward Thanatos embedded within a cyberpositive system, is indexed by Land to, among other things, the dynamics of the market. Consider this fragment from "Meltdown," a presentation from 1994:

16. Nick Land, "Machinic Desire," *Textural Practice* 7, no. 3 (1993): 478, 480, reprinted as Nick Land, "Machinic Desire," in *Fanged Noumena: Collected Writings 1987–2007* (Falmouth, U.K.: Urbanomic, 2011), 337, 340. On a personal note, in going back to this text of Land's, I realized that I had quoted from it on my blog on the very day of the Flash Crash.

17. Nick Land, "No Future," in *Fanged Noumena*, 397.

Neoclassical (equilibrium) economics is subsumed into computer-based nonequilibrium market escalations, themed by artificial agencies, imperfect information, sub-optimal solutions, lock-in, increasing returns, and convergence. As digitally micro-tuned market metaprograms mesh with technoscientific soft engineering, cyberpositive nonlinearity rages through the machines. Cyclonic torsion moans.[18]

My own evocation of Land through voluminous quoting from his work is meant not only to note a certain *prescience* in his writings but also, as with Lyotard, to re-present the dynamics of his writing, a dynamics that follows the noisiness of his referents. Land's writing resonates with the activity of computational technologies, of their fits and starts and seeming ability to act in ways that exceed their rational, ordered frameworks. And what are the "microtuned market metaprograms" but the algorithms of AT or HFT? The body of Land's work from the 1990s deserves its own reactivation during a time when the imbrication of computational technologies—of electronic trading, of mathematical formalism—seems to have run amok. Though we may be profoundly concerned about the *implications* of Land's seeming disavowal of human agency to intervene within cyberpositive systems, we perhaps should understand these texts as the speculative imaginary of a delirious merging of theory and fiction that mirrors the purported fusion of human and machine. I read Land's writings against the grain, not as prescriptions to be enacted, nor a political position to be held, but rather as oneric possibilities that mark some of the fundamental implications of the theories, authors, and materials we hold dear.

Nevertheless, Noys has returned to his critique of accelerationism in his recent book *Malign Velocities: Accelerationism*

18. Nick Land, "Meltdown," in ibid., 447.

and Capitalism. Here Noys understands accelerationism, in the form in which it is currently expressed, as a "fantasy of smooth integration" of humans, machines, and capital.[19] Noys is fundamentally concerned, among other things, with what he sees as the transformation of misery into *jouissance,* as indexed by the quotation from Lyotard earlier.[20] Instead, Noys wants to restore "the sense of friction that interrupts and disrupts" the aforementioned fantasy.[21] Yet I would argue that there is no necessary reason to eschew accelerationism for this alone. I read under the surface of Land's texts a graininess, a noisiness that interferes with the seemingly smooth fantasy he presents. Indeed, fantasy is never as straightforward as it seems. As previously mentioned, I see accelerationists such as Land presenting a speculative fantasy, not a political program. And fantasy is needed more than ever to help us develop new conceptual apparatuses out of the "there is no alternative" doldrums. Shaviro understands this as well when he writes that "science fiction is the accelerationist art *par excellence.*"[22]

Perhaps what is problematic, then, is understanding this fantasy as a set of guidelines for future behavior. If we cannot assume that accelerating capitalism will cause it to collapse under its own contradictions (something that has not yet occurred, and something that we have no reason to expect *will* occur), then can we develop a properly accelerationist program? Or should we rather see it more as an aesthetic movement, as Shaviro does? Alex Williams and Nick Srnicek attempt to lay out one potential program in their "#Accelerate: Manifesto for

19. Benjamin Noys, *Malign Velocities: Accelerationism and Capitalism* (Alresford, U.K.: Zero Books, 2014), 103.

20. Ibid., 101.

21. Ibid., 103.

22. Shaviro, *No Speed Limit,* 3.

an Accelerationist Politics."[23] Williams and Srnicek do not accept the Lyotardian or Landian joy at being consumed by capital, at being torn apart by machines physical and digital; rather, they argue that we need to be at ease with the technologies of capital and thus figure out how to repurpose them for more progressive ends—in short, there is no return to a pastoral, pre-Fordist life. But like Shaviro, I am troubled by their call for a "Promethean politics of maximal mastery over society and its environment."[24] The masculinist and, frankly, colonial connotations of their call for "mastery" ignore the potential enjoyment of being merged with and/or submissive to the machine. Why should these possibilities be rejected tout court? There can be joy in being utterly consumed by a machine in a way that does not simultaneously require an acceptance of the violence that machines do to people on a daily basis. But more importantly, Williams and Srnicek's desire for "mastery" ignores the ways in which machines function in fashions unintended by their creators—and we do not have to make an obligatory reference to *The Terminator* (dir. James Cameron, 1984) to understand this. Instead, we need to understand in minute detail the *dynamics* of how humans, machines, and capitalism come together in a nexus, to discover the potential fissures that constitute the bases for new potential configurations, rather than attempt a "mastery" that preexists this nexus.

So as a result, I would also have to reject Williams and Srnicek's call for a "universal accelerationism" where the "cunning automata" of HFT "are liberated from the capital-

23. Alex Williams and Nick Srnicek, "#Accelerate: Manifesto for an Accelerationist Politics," in Mackay and Avanessian, *#ACCELERATE#*, 347–62.

24. Ibid., 360. For Shaviro's critiques, see *No Speed Limit*, 16–20.

ist dynamic."[25] Here they suggest that such a liberation would "direct capitalism towards a sequence of terminal secular crises" that would produce a "properly post-capitalist society."[26] Srnicek and Williams suggest that there is a "contingency of the universal," but I would argue that it is precisely this contingency, what I call noise, that prevents their universal accelerationism from ever occurring. For as we have seen throughout this essay, noise has more often than not brought these "cyberpositive" systems of HFT into equilibrium. Without this correcting force—a force that is not in a realm divorced from humans but rather is because of the ecology of practices and approaches to algorithmic trading—we would have seen the stock market tank to zero on days like May 6, 2010. But this did not occur, precisely because there is no "universal accelerationism" at work due to the functioning of noise. The market is made up of billions of local decisions being made, decisions that are in all cases affected, at least in part, by human thought and action and by the vicissitudes of the material world. Yet these decisions are not necessarily predictable, again due to noise: everything from the noise of an errant cosmic ray upsetting a bit in the memory of a computer to the incorrect inputting of a sell order. As there is no universal, omniscient standpoint in the market that would allow one to perfectly predict the outcome of these algorithmic potential decisions, we can never control, nor guide, a "universal accelerationism," and a "Promethean politics" is impossible.[27]

25. Nick Srnicek and Alex Williams, "On Cunning Automata: Financial Acceleration at the Limits of the Dromological," *Collapse* 8 (2014).

26. Ibid.

27. As Shaviro notes, even for Marx, "a tendency is always accompanied by 'counteracting factors' which can inhibit or even reverse it." See

Likewise, Plant and Land's "cyberpositive" can never occur within the systems that exist in our world. Like the dynamics of chaotic systems, small fluctuations can cause a switch into negative feedback, reestablishing stability. The eschatology of Land's texts indexes a desire; but desire remains wedded to material practices that are not entirely amenable to desire's own machinations. As I have shown in this essay, noise can be counted on for only one thing: an excess that escapes containment within tactics or strategies of positive *or* negative determination. Noise needs to be understood within its dynamics of *both* cyberpositive and cybernegative systems, and thus its progressive micropolitical potentials need to be heard simultaneously with the possibility of near-instantaneous shifts toward regressive registers.

So if noise prevents accelerationism from occurring, what is the point of accelerationism? I agree with Patricia Reed that we should instead conceptualize accelerationism as a reorientation, a *need* to direct "existing energies in (as yet) inexistent directions": "It is precisely here, on this kernel of stasis, that the call to accelerate needs to take hold, dislodging stagnant conceptual orientations in favor of the creation of eccentric, out-of-centre attractors, where we may discover trajectories of a vectorial (and not rotational or circulatory) sort."[28] Accelerationism is a fantasy, but it is a fantasy that has enabled us to begin to speculate about the future again. We thus need to recapture the term *speculation* from the world of finance, to remove it from the boring domain of continual attempts to accumulate capital:

Shaviro, *No Speed Limit*, 3.

28. Patricia Reed, "Seven Prescriptions for Accelerationism," in Mackay and Avanessian, *#ACCELERATE#*, 524, 525.

To speculate is to articulate and enable the contingencies of the given, armed only with the certainty that what is, is always incomplete; to speculate is to play with the demonstration of this innately porous, nontotalisable set of givens. Extricating "speculation" from its current bedfellow of finance entails a fidelity to an incalculable future divorced from the reductive apparatus of the wager, wherein all possibilities are conflated with probabilities.[29]

Such a call resonates with Franco "Bifo" Berardi's interest in "poetry" as a way to combat the financialization of language.[30] So we can work from Land and Lyotard's heretical texts not with the goal of implementing and realizing their visions but rather as speculations of their own. We can speculate as well, and speculate how to cope with the world as it is presently arranged. From coping we can move forward, articulating the fissures that allow us, at least locally, to shape the nexus of humans, machines, and capital toward desires that are not subsumed by the market. Speculation, poetry, futurity: rather than acceleration toward a given goal, instead the tactile construction of trajectories that respect the noisiness of materiality and that do not have a teleology.

29. Ibid., 527.
30. Berardi, *Uprising*.

Glossary

arbitrage
In short, first the identification of a discrepancy between the price of a security and what it "should" be, according to fundamental analysis or technical analysis, and then the exploitation of this discrepancy for the capture of profit. Arbitrage can be conducted in a number of ways, depending on the market or the security. See, e.g., statistical arbitrage.

arbitrageur
One who engages in arbitrage.

ask
Lowest price a seller is willing to accept for a security.

bid
Highest price a buyer is willing to pay for a security.

direct market access
Exchange technologies that enable so-called buy-side firms direct access to the order book of an exchange, bypassing sell-side firms or their own in-house brokers.

E-Mini S&P
Index futures product linked to the S&P 500 Index. The contract trades at $50 times the value of the index. Recent volumes of the contract were upward of 1.8 million meaning the value of daily trades is more than $120 billion.

fundamental analysis
Form of financial analysis based on so-called fundamental properties of a security, such as a firm's profit, its performance in relationship to the performance of other firms in its market segment, and broader changes in the economy (e.g., interest rates). See also technical analysis.

limit order book
The list of open limit orders consisting of the set of bids and asks. The limit order book has often been available only to specialists and/or market makers and therefore not visible to the public. With the move to direct market access, so-called buy-side investors are now able to interact with the limit order book without the need for an intervening broker.

noise trader
One who is assumed to be unable to distinguish between "valid" and "invalid" information within a market. Although noise traders should not be able to survive within a market owing to the quick exhaustion of their capital, recent models and empirical evidence have shown otherwise.

open-outcry trading
Material and bodily form of trading whereby offers to buy or sell a security are settled through specific hand motions and vocal shouts. In the Chicago Board of Trade, such activity is done in the "pits," a series of raised steps that also determines position within the social hierarchy of traders. Such trading has diminished greatly in importance with the rise of electronic communication networks.

proprietary trading
Trading conducted with the firm's own capital rather than with the capital contributed by its clients.

security
A financial asset that can be traded. Common securities include stocks (shares in a corporation), bonds (a debt that must be paid with interest), and derivatives. As long as one can "package" an asset into something that can be traded, and there is a market for buying and selling it, one can create a security.

spread
The difference in price between the bid and the ask.

statistical arbitrage
See technical analysis.

technical analysis
Form of financial analysis based on observable properties of market data, such as the temporal sequence of the price and volume of a security, that aims to understand how such data fit into previously defined patterns that might suggest future changes in the security. In its most advanced form, technical analysis develops a statistical model based on prior data to predict future movements. When a deviation from this model is found, it is a potential arbitrage opportunity, leading to the term statistical arbitrage, a key technique in high-frequency trading. See also fundamental analysis.

Acknowledgments

I wrote much of this essay while at the Cornell University Society for the Humanities during the year on "Sound: Culture, Theory, Practice, Politics"; thanks to everyone there for his or her excellent feedback and support. Steven Shaviro and Bernard Geoghegan provided needed comments and encouragement. Phoebe Sengers, Tim Murray, María Fernández, and Tarleton Gillespie shepherded the project in its early stages. An anonymous reviewer helped tighten my argument. Earlier versions were presented at the Society for Literature, Science, and the Arts (SLSA), the Stevens Institute of Technology, the Pratt Institute, SUNY Buffalo, and Wellesley College. Claudia Pederson has been there since the beginning.

Nicholas A. Knouf is assistant professor of cinema and media studies at Wellesley College in Wellesley, Massachusetts.